D1742923

Produced by:
Quintessentially Publishing Ltd.
29 Portland Place
London, W1B 1QB
Tel: +44 (0)203 073 6799
Fax: +44 (0)207 692 0213
www.quintessentiallypublishing.com

Design by:
Quintessentially Design Ltd.
Tel: +44 (0)20 7758 3331

No part of this book may be reproduced or transmitted electronically or mechanically,
including photocopying without permission of the publisher.

Copyright ©2011 by Quintessentially Publishing Ltd.
All rights reserved.

QUINTESSENTIALLY PUBLISHING

QUINTESSENTIALLY RESERVE
Featuring 150 of the most sought-after and unique global travel destinations.
www.quintessentiallyreserve.com

QUINTESSENTIALLY PURE
A collection of 100 of the most beautiful spas in the world.
www.quintessentiallypure.com

QUINTESSENTIALLY LIVING
A stunning art book and directory of everything needed for the luxury home.
www.quintessentiallyliving.com

QUINTESSENTIALLY PERFUME
A beautiful insight into the world's most inspired, innovative and authentic perfumes.

QUBE
The social networking site for Quintessentially members and their friends.
www.qubers.com

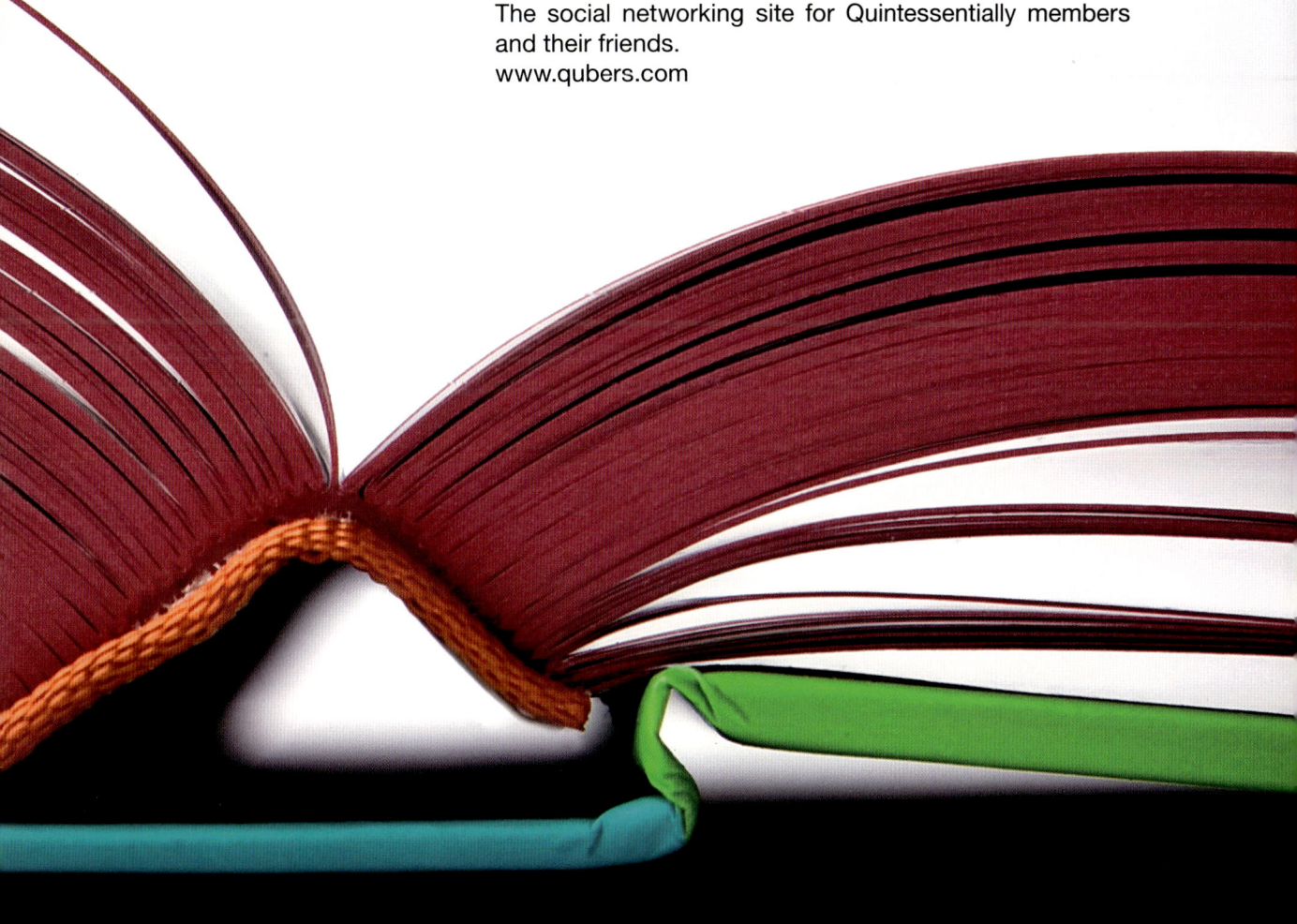

QUINTESSENTIALLY
HOME

HOME ORGANISATION · ERRAND RUNNING · CLEANERS ELECTRICIANS · PLUMBERS · HANDYMEN · ARCHITECTS · STAFF EMPLOYMENT · HOME MANAGEMENT · INTERIOR DESIGN

Quintessentially Home can cover all of your home needs using our specialist onsite staff and a reliable team of London based runners.

With expert knowledge and an extensive list of qualified suppliers on hand 24 hours a day, this comprehensive service is a sure way to make your life that much easier and more productive, giving you more time to spend as you wish.

Welcome to Quintessentially Living Vol. II

Quintessentially Publishing is thrilled to bring you the second volume of Quintessentially Living.

Our first edition lovingly and expertly created by Anton Mossa opened a window onto the world of interior design and ignited curiosity amongst our readers and Quintessentially members. This second volume was a natural sequel which would continue the exploration and also pay tribute to up-and-coming designers.

The book contains a wealth of designers to introduce, whose works are striking, groundbreaking and of course, luxurious. Those we have revisited have fresh collections which we feel sure you will find as inspiring as we have throughout this process.

Our Living Insider chapter offers an insight into the lives of some creative and enterprising individuals and companies whose star is on the ascent. Additionally our article on the Benjamin Franklin House reveals the fascinating details of this restored building and we hope it will whet your appetite to take time to visit it and observe the craftsmanship involved in this surprising project first hand.

This book will draw your eye to the finer details which make each and every designer stand out from the crowd with their blend of character and invention. This book will also have a life outside the immediate world of Quintessentially as it will be sold in book and lifestyle stores, making it available to design experts and novices alike. So sit back and immerse yourself in the pages that follow.

ANNABELLA NASSETTI
A LIVING CONCEPT

Since 1997, Annabella has cracked the market in stylish, innovative and practical interior design with Annabella Nassetti Ltd. This is only the beginning however. Annabella takes the experience of creating the ultimate living space even further.

In harnessing the expertise of a sister company - the construction business AN Building and Maintenance Ltd (or ANBM Ltd) - Annabella ensures that every aspect of creation and implementation is dealt with in synergy with Annabella Nassetti Ltd. The latter will synthesize the design and technical rigours of interior architecture to reinvent her clients' living space. Then ANBM Ltd, a team of in-house builders, all of whom are selected as like-minded and passionate professionals, carry out construction, fitting and refurbishment to guarantee reliability and quality of execution. Direct and constant communication with project managers and designers from their fellow sister company guarantees fuss-free success and efficiency. This valuable asset is Annabella's trump card; it makes for a smooth working process and it has attracted business from external interior designers whose reliance on professional engineers and experts is of paramount importance. In addition ANBM Ltd can act as consultants in all aspects of property refurbishment, from listed buildings to planning consent to bespoke specialist solutions, thereby ensuring crucial support to the designer and the property owner and there is also a 'post-production' maintenance service for clients.

Practicality will never overshadow style however and Annabella's personal style permeates all her work from living spaces right through to exciting boat designs she is commissioned for. Luxurious textures, finishes and architectural details as well as sophisticated technology, personalised colour schemes and finishing touches can and do transform her clients' aspirations into elegant reality. As Annabella admits simply: "It seems to be a very good formula and so far it is keeping us very busy."

Photography by Heike Bohnstengel

For further information and requests please find all contact details in the index pages 172-175

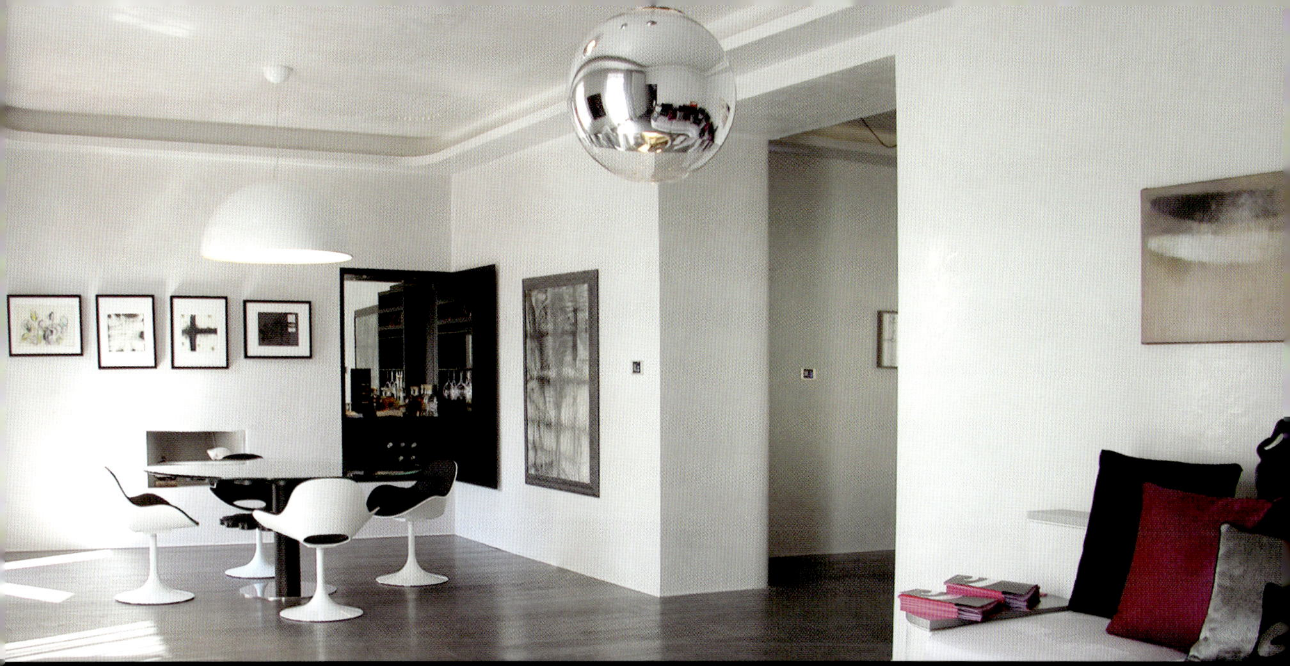

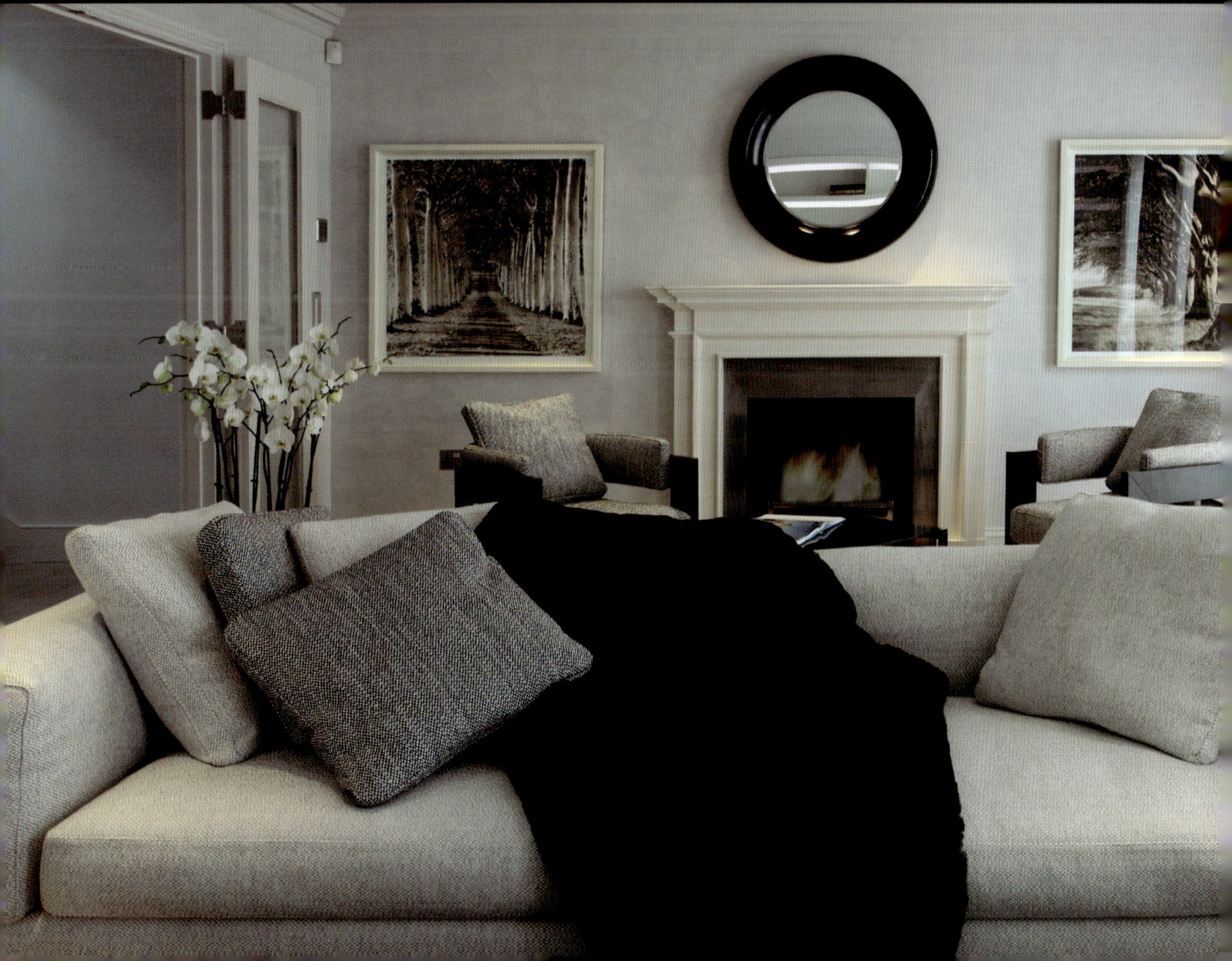

ANNA CASA INTERIORS

Bold coloured-glass walls and floors form a modernist backdrop to a highly select range of dramatic, sculptural, statement furniture in Anna Dodonova's destination showroom, Anna Casa Interiors, an inspiring space to be found in London's Chelsea Harbour. Established in the Design Centre in 2007, Anna Casa Interiors was personally designed by Anna to showcase a harmonious range of interior designs.

A glamorous individual with great personal style of her own, Anna personally chooses each of the dramatic pieces of furniture on show, curated from a stable of prominent international brands. Anna's background in art and graphic design is evident in the sleek, colourful, modern interior of the showroom, as is her love of strong, clean lines in Italian design. But her inspiration and influences extend far further than Europe. 'I travel all around the world for inspiration' says the globetrotting designer, 'and I find design ideas everywhere and in everything I see'.

Furnishings range from sparkling chandeliers, unique, handmade Murano glass dining tables, ultra-luxurious beds, sideboards and tables in hardwoods and metals and bespoke, wonderfully tactile soft furnishings.

Anna also provides an interior designer service for select customers on high-end residential, hotel and commercial projects around the world. Her background and training in interior, graphic and art design allows her to explore many different styles and mediums of furniture and design. Added to this, her keen eye for detail, creative vision and personal approach means each project is a reflection of the personality and lifestyle of the customer and made to their own specifications. The showroom is an invaluable asset to Anna's interior design clients and her team offers a full professional sourcing service supplying bespoke items not only from Anna Casa but other companies and contacts worldwide.

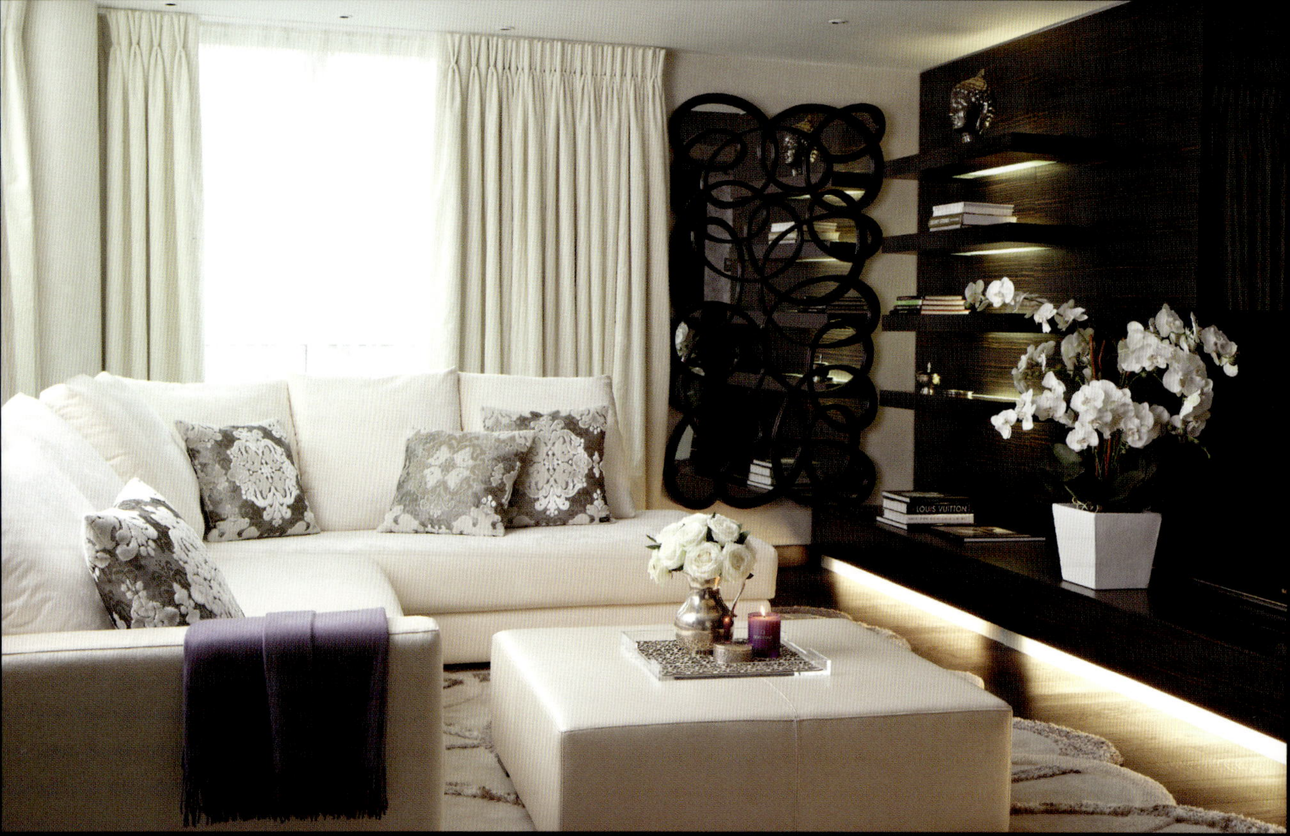
LOUIS VUITTON

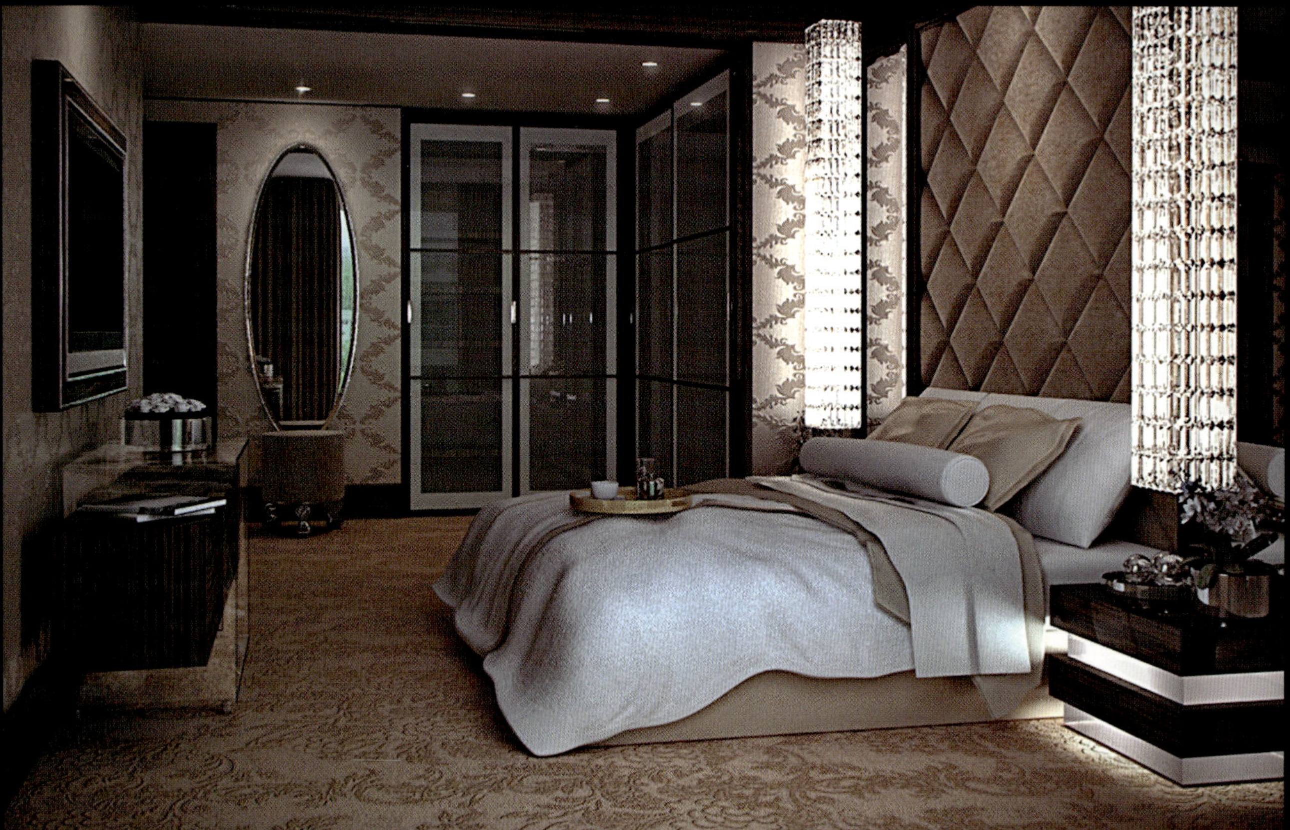

BISQUE

Bisque has singlehandedly revolutionised our perception of the radiator as a simple functional requirement. They have transformed the radiator into a living, working piece of art. This exciting and innovative company creates an impressive range of designs from spectacular, statement pieces for large spaces to sleek, space-saving towel radiators and compact school-style models. With an unrivalled imagination and a vast portfolio of products, Bisque accommodates bespoke sizes, over 2000 colours as well as a complementary colour matching service to coordinate radiators with existing décor. Unusual finishes are one of Bisque's hallmarks, including individually etched brass or copper, textured quartz and iridescent, two-tone colours.

With an enviable reputation and numerous international awards to its name, Bisque's designs have been exhibited in the London Design Museum and the Philadelphia Museum of Modern Art. However, the spirit of the company is very much alive and thrives on an organic and continuous renewal of stock from world class designers sourced regularly for their outstanding creations bursting with colour and character - the unique Italian-made wooden models are recent notable additions to the collection.

Bisque stands out in the industry notably because of the superior manufacturing quality of its cutting edge styles combined with a good old fashioned approach to service and meticulous attention to detail. Bisque boasts stunning showrooms in London and Bath but also a gorgeous website which showcases a comprehensive guide to the range, including sections on kitchens, bathrooms and matching valves – you can even customise your ideal radiator online complete with colour and size.

Next time you are thinking of how to warm and adorn your living space you'd be hard pushed to find a finer example of inventive practicality than Bisque.

BRAHM INTERIORS

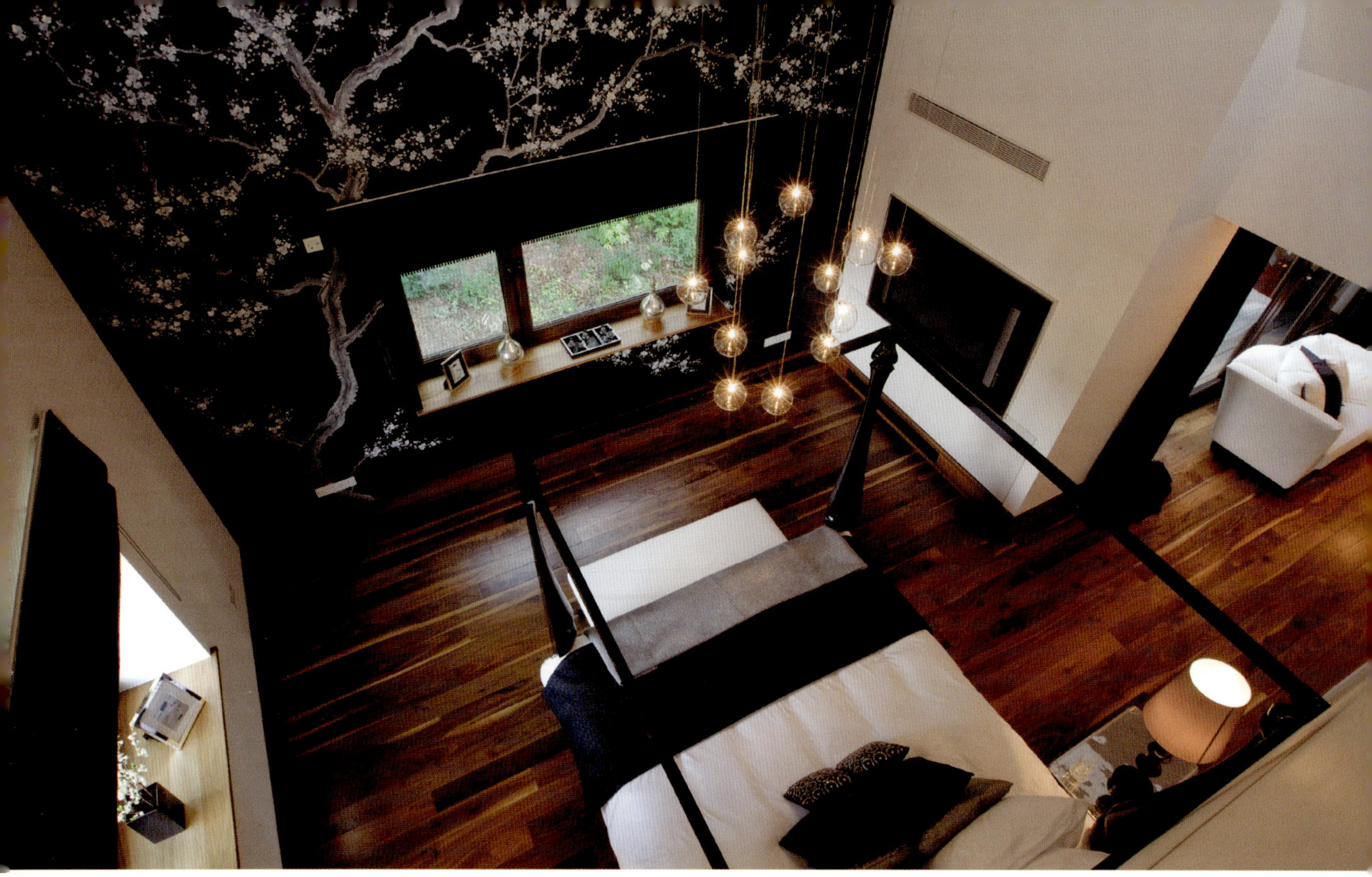

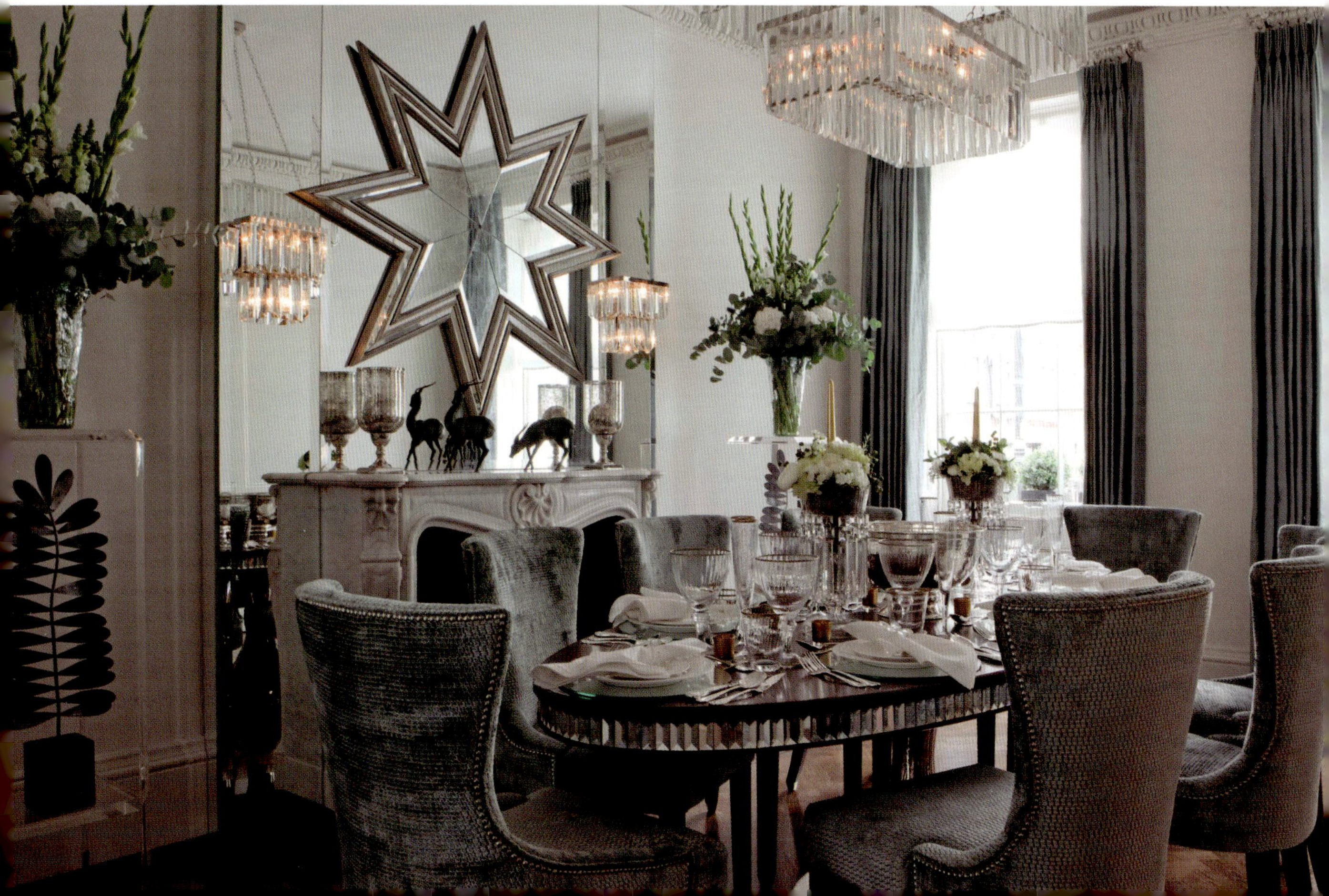

Based in the heart of Belgravia, interior design company Brahm Interiors defines opulent spaces that whisper refined, contemporary grandeur and effortless chic. The company was founded by Pierre Brahm whose singular taste, vision and uncompromising standards have paved the way for the firm's extraordinary success. In a remarkable first decade of business, Pierre and his designers have deservedly received accolades that include a Design and Decoration Award for Best Show Home, being shortlisted for a British Interior Design Award and a coveted nomination for Interior Designer of the Year at the first annual Quintessentially Awards.

En route to being recognised as leaders of the London high-end interiors scene, Brahm Interiors have tailor-made environments for a portfolio of discerning and design-conscious clientele across a variety of properties worldwide. Projects have included an historic castle in Kent, a lavish Belgravia mews house, an ultramodern abode on Billionaire's Row and a sensational roof terrace in the heart of Knightsbridge.

Property developers have seen rental yields significantly increased by utilising the transformative abilities of Brahm's talented creative team. They are delighted to help with all aspects of building the perfect home, stepping in to consult on everything from sourcing collections of fine art to recommending schools and gyms in the local area. Private clients have experienced service that is so reliable and beautifully bespoke they can even trust the company with picking out books for their newly installed library. It is testament to how in-tune Brahm Interiors are with the needs of their clientele that they can offer lifestyle management services such as these. Inspiration and intuition for luxury living is all it takes to achieve the ideal home, and Brahm Interiors have that rare gift.

BROOSK SAIB

Vibrant, sumptuous and individual, the interiors designed by Baghdad-born designer Broosk Saib are anything but bland. Ranging from the richly historical to the starkly contemporary, the designs that he has generated over the course of his 25 year career maintain an opulent standard of luxury, whatever their style.

Moving to England as teenager, Broosk did not plan to become an interior designer at all but began studying business at the American College in London, where the diverse range of elective courses on offer allowed his introduction to the medium. By 1985 he had his first office in Knightsbridge, moving on to a showroom on Fulham Road shortly afterwards, he now works from his home in South West London, which he believes best demonstrates his personal flair for creating strictly bespoke, elegant and stylish interiors.

Eyeing each new space that he tackles as a 'stage set', Broosk has been described as 'lively' by those he has worked with, and is marked out as a designer who does not shy away from exciting commissions and demanding clients. Whether it's a swaggering bachelor pad in Notting Hill, a cosy pied à terre in St Tropez or a glittering, hidden gem of a bolt hole in Marrakech, Broosk is inspired to make something new each time.

His love of conventional English decorative elements is married with a fresh, international taste in textiles, antiques and colour schemes, resulting in spaces that have varying levels of exotic theatricality. Unusual materials such as bone, fur and wood run throughout his work, as do rich specialist finishes such as playfully monogrammed bespoke wallpaper, frescoed ceilings and trompe l'oeil paint effects. The softening effects of drapery and clever techniques, like casually stacking up coffee table books on sumptuously upholstered ottomans, make his rooms both aesthetically ideal and yet cosily lived-in. Mantle pieces display an assembly of objects that look lovingly collected and lighting schemes are always soft, sympathetic and carefully composed. Broosk Saib is undoubtedly a designer of evident depths.

CAROLYN TREVOR DESIGN

Architects and interior designers can make uneasy bedfellows - both vying to realise a creative vision that might not necessarily be mutual - but at Carolyn Trevor Design, there is no such professional tension. A trained architect herself, Carolyn has set up an interior design practice that complements the work of Trevor Lahiff Architects, the practice she runs with her husband Pat Lahiff: same office, same ideas, and no disharmony.

Beyond the obvious benefit for clients - only having one design professional to deal with during the long and often complex business of shaping a new home - it also means a creative coherence and an approach to interior design that is as precise as you would expect from someone with an architectural background. Carolyn's superior draughtsmanship was embedded during nearly a decade working for renowned residential expert John Stefanidis. His practice having a reputation not just for being one of the hardest working in the business, but the most prestigious - her time there included a two-year spell living on a Welsh hillside while the team worked on the interiors for Eaton Hall, the Cheshire home of the Duke of Westminster. Setting up on her own in 1997, Carolyn's architectural practice expanded to include interior design as well, either as stand-alone projects or in conjunction with the company' sin-house architects.

Understanding how fundamentally one's living space affects an individual's everyday life is central to the philosophy of innovative design firm Casa Forma, who have made it their mission to positively impact the environments and lives of each and every one of their clients by creating a home that reflects their individuality, personality, lifestyle and personal style.

Formed in 2007 by way of a creative collaboration between award winning architect and interior designer Luigi Esposito, and successful serial entrepreneur Faiza Seth, Casa Forma has rapidly grown into a thriving high-end architectural design firm with headquarters in London. Their particular brand of faultlessly tasteful, elegant, yet warm and livable interiors has attracted a discerning clientele comprised of Russian oligarchs, celebrities, Middle Eastern royalty, industrialist Indian families, and other successful entrepreneurs. Casa Forma's portfolio includes many high end residential properties in Mayfair, Knightsbridge, Belgravia and Chelsea, commercial projects including retail stores in Chelsea and Saville Row, a gorgeous private polo club in Berkshire and a couple of sprawling countryside mansions to boot.

Busy they may be, but Casa Forma takes the time to get to know clients intimately, believing that the best service is achieved through a collaborative process of designing, focusing first on optimizing the functionality of a space, after which interior design is then lovingly applied.

Whether it's a private residence or a commercial space, Casa Forma aims to enhance properties through innovative design, improved layout and increased functionality. Drawing on each client's personal lifestyle, their design team creates the ultimate environment by combining comfort with luxury and functionality with finish.

Moon Onyx cladded to entrance foyer walls with back lighting adds subtle glow. Bronze trims frame the onyx to create the feel of a piece of art.

Designed with exceptional materials including selection of natural stained walnut, ebonized and macassar timbers.

The entrance floor leading to corridor consists of "Biancone Perlino Anticato Reale" stone with trims and details in bronze.

| Melted bronze and silver sheets of metal cladded to feature walls harmonise with ebonised macassar panelling.

CHARLIE YORK LIMITED

Graced with an outstanding eye for texture, composition and finish, combined with the finest contemporary printing, mounting and framing techniques, Charlie York Limited produce unique, decorative works for both corporate and private clients that seek to reconnect inside space with the natural environment, sparking debate and creating an atmosphere of original distinction. With their intriguing in-house images as a basis, Charlie York Limited offer a bespoke design service where the client's personal preferences are accommodated, forming unmatched and exclusive collections.

After an initial consultation, a tailor-made portfolio is created from which choices of image, style and finish are discussed; and with quality and service of paramount importance, aided by a constant dialogue with their clients, Charlie York Limited pride themselves on producing pieces that exceed satisfaction.

Photographer and designer John Rose founded Charlie York Limited to provide bespoke, wall-hung design pieces that explore our relationship with natural design. Combining his skill for photography with an excellent eye for creating client led design pieces, John Rose and Charlie York Limited produce works celebrating the complex beauty of the familiar that are uniquely tailored to the client's requirements.

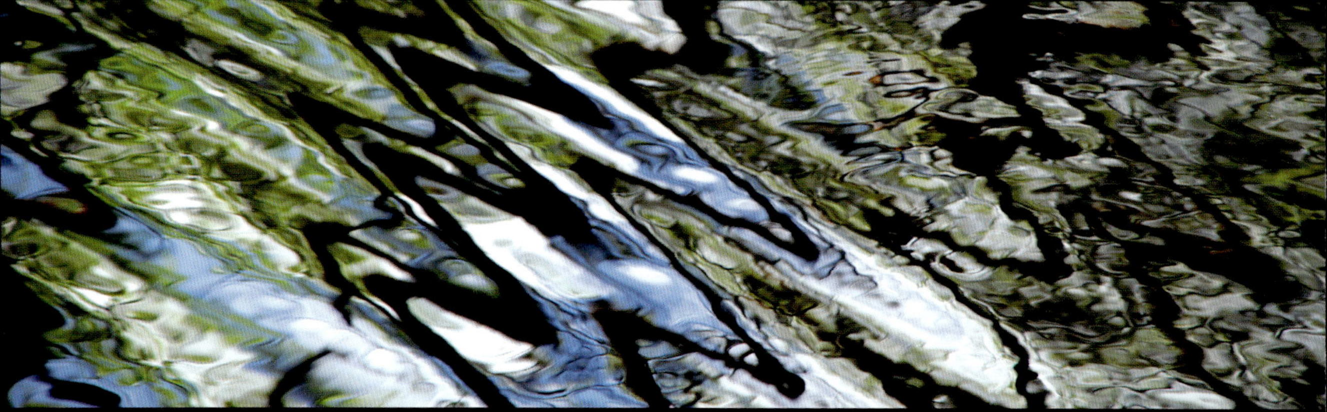

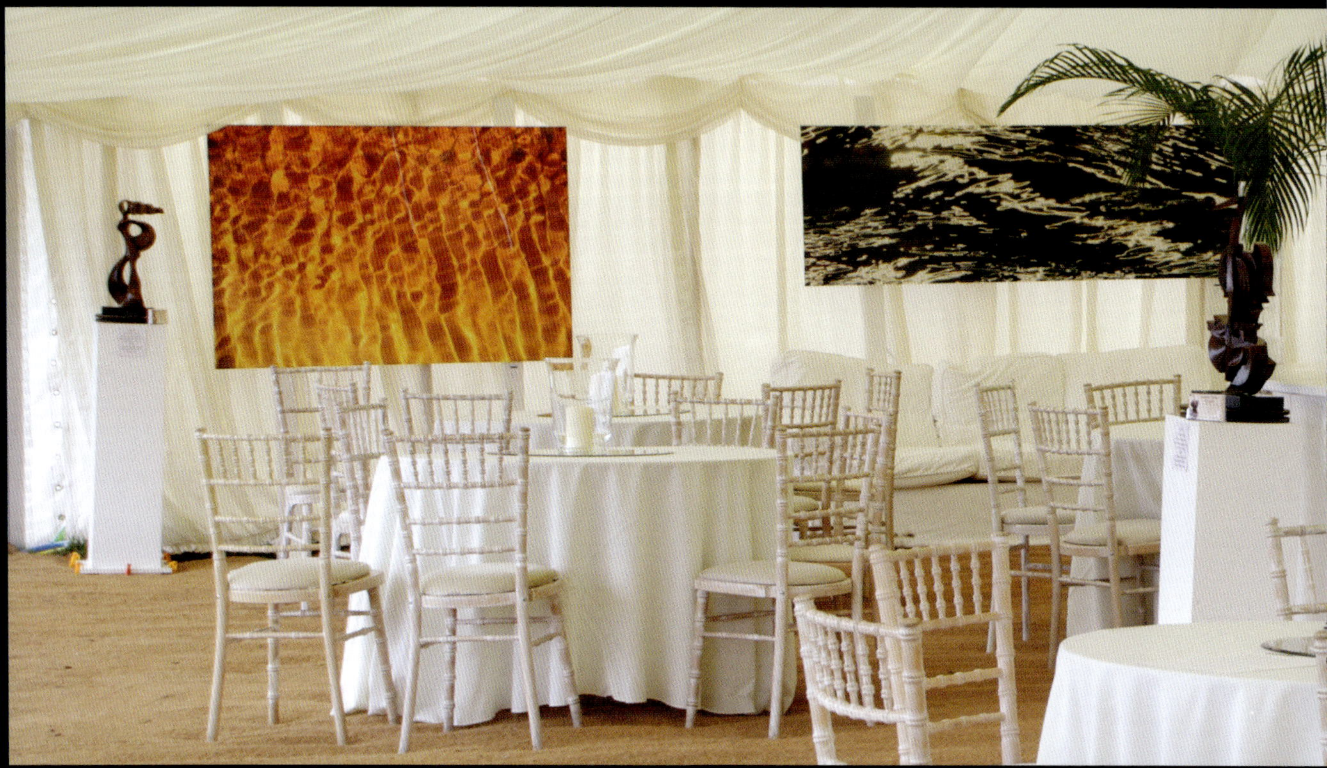

COLLECTION PIERRE

With influences spanning the ages from Pharaonic Egypt to Antiquity and inspirations drawn from the sumptuous curvilinear styles of the Art Deco Movement to the clean lines of 21st Century design, artisanal furniture company Collection Pierre has a rich and eclectic aesthetic heritage with a company history to match.

In 1930, Pierre Counot-Blandin established his own cabinet-making workshop in the Vosges region of France. Pierre, the grandfather of Collection Pierre co-founder Gaëtan d'Hôtel, worked with master craftsmen such as Ruhlmann, Arbus and Leleu and, as a team of cabinetmakers they became famous for crafting the Normandie ocean liner's elegant first-class lounge furniture. Enveloped by 2,000 hectares of dense beech forest, Pierre's remote workshop soon became known for its accurate replicas of 17th, 18th and 19th century furniture styles. Today, each Collection Pierre piece is still painstakingly handcrafted and finished in the original Counot-Blandin workshop by cabinetmakers, sculptors, marquetry-makers, gilders, lacquerers, upholsterers and tapestry-makers whose traditional methods have been passed down through generations.

The designs aim to capture the elegance of classic French furniture design while redefining it for modern 21st century tastes. The Collection's original designer, John Hutton, who launched the collection with Gaëtan d'Hôtel and Marc Bonnet in 2005, established the exacting principles of elegance for which the collection is now so well known. The current designer Jean-Louis Deniot follows in his footsteps, bringing a fresh purity and rigour to this vision. Collection Pierre's designers are concerned with more than just the look of their pieces, however. Doctors, chiropractors and physiotherapists are consulted to ensure that each chair, bed or ottoman offers adequate support for healthy postures. With accommodating the individual needs of their clients in mind, Collection Pierre also offers a bespoke service that is based on the Pierre Archives, covering the periods from Louis XIII to the 19th Century and Art Deco, where uniquely adapted pieces can be made to order.

Collection Pierre opened their first UK showroom on Bourne Street in June 2009 and the store not only sells the Collection itself, but also a range of exceptional bronze and crystal chandeliers and light fittings by French specialists Par Excellence. Collection Pierre is the exclusive European distributor for John Hutton Textiles, a collection of fabrics that are sophisticated, glamorous and incredibly versatile. The company is already popular with prestigious interior designers who use furniture from the range in both private houses and hotel-commissioned design schemes. Examples can be seen at Claridges in London, George V and the Plaza Athenee in Paris, Cheval Blanc in Courchevel and recently completed projects include both the restaurant and bar at the Savoy Hotel in London, and the Shangri La Hotel in Paris. So, if you were to indulge in one of their pieces or luxurious decorative schemes, you know that your house would be in very good company indeed.

DAVI**D**SON

Since Davidson first made impressive steps into the world of furniture design, experts and fans throughout the UK and worldwide have eagerly anticipated their every move. With an in house team of experts that prides itself on a service that is so personalised, yielding such excellent results, Davidson has become the first and only creator of choice for many private clients and important global interior designers. The company specialises in high calibre dining tables, side cabinets, occasional and console tables as well as dining chairs and accessories. This portfolio of work is well suited to high end luxury hotels, super yachts and boardrooms while the team provides a made to measure service for any project or room size. Clients can select the timber and dimensions of their choice through the aid of 2D and 3D drawings, quotations and timber samples. They can alternatively opt for standard specifications and have their dining table made to fit any number of people.

One of Davidson's most notable strengths is the ability to produce stunning, clean and classic lines graced with modern twist. The results are unique, elegant and timeless. Never content to rest on their enviable laurels, this innovative company approaches every new season, every new piece with vigour and a taste for the unexpected. There's one thing you can be sure of - Davidson will be leading the way and making waves in the world of interior design for generations to come.

ENGLISH GEORGIAN

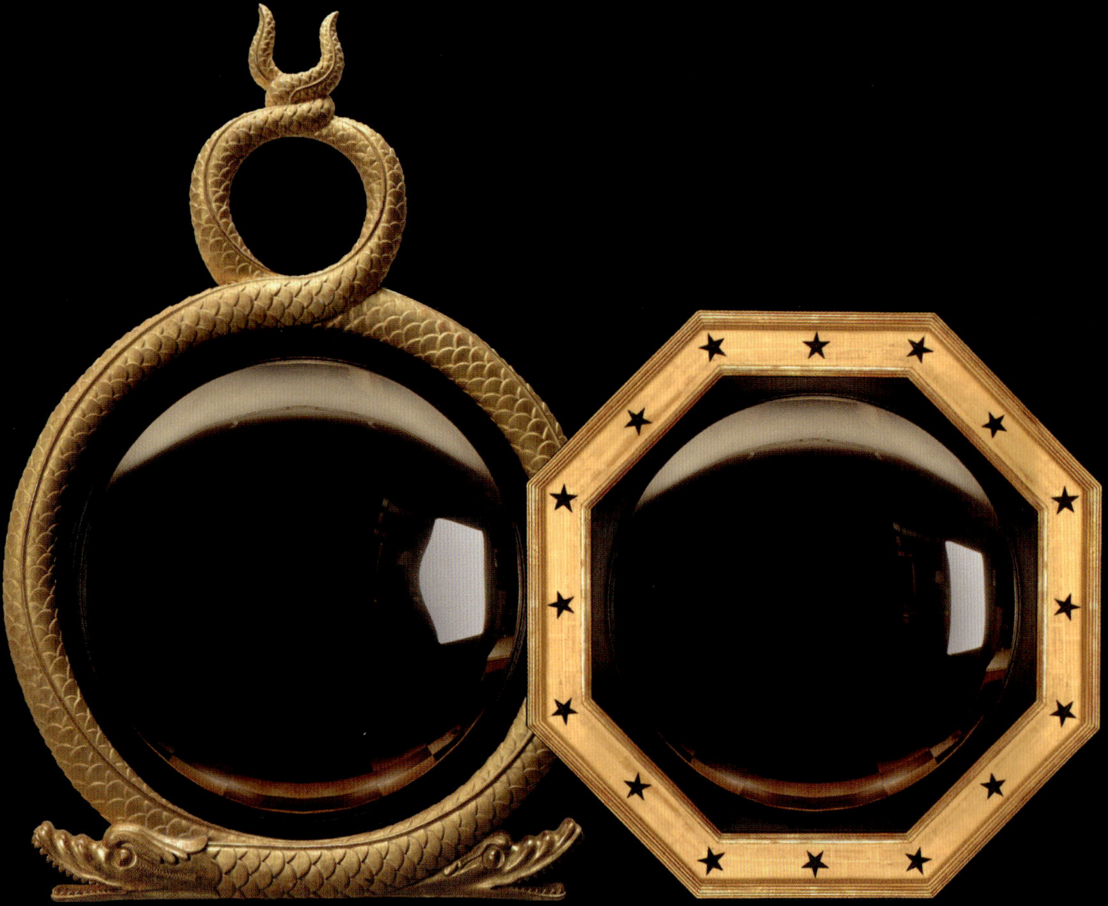

English Georgian is a highly respected company based in the prestigious Design Centre Chelsea Harbour. Their work however extends around the world and this is reflected in the designs they exhibit in their showrooms across the USA and Moscow.

Clients worldwide have come to trust and admire the level of authenticity they bring to their work thanks to a meticulous attention to detail that only authentic craftsmanship can allow for. From hand carved mirrors to furniture, their designs are of the finest quality and the finished product makes for a home that is wholly personalised. Inspired by the great names of English furniture design, English Georgian produces an extensive range of products of unsurpassed quality and style.

The team at English Georgian has the skills and experience necessary to work in collaboration with their clients to produce beautiful bespoke pieces.

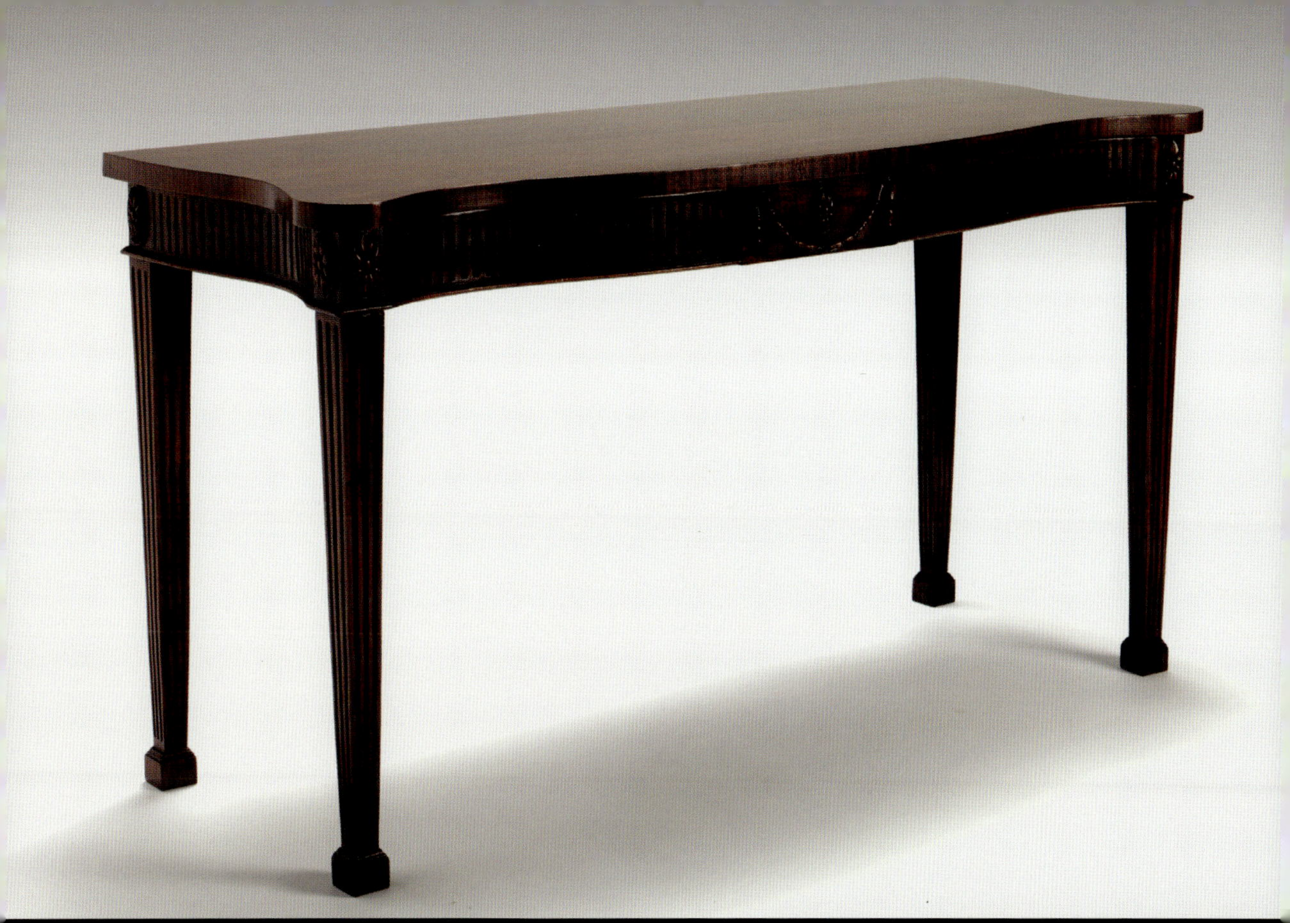
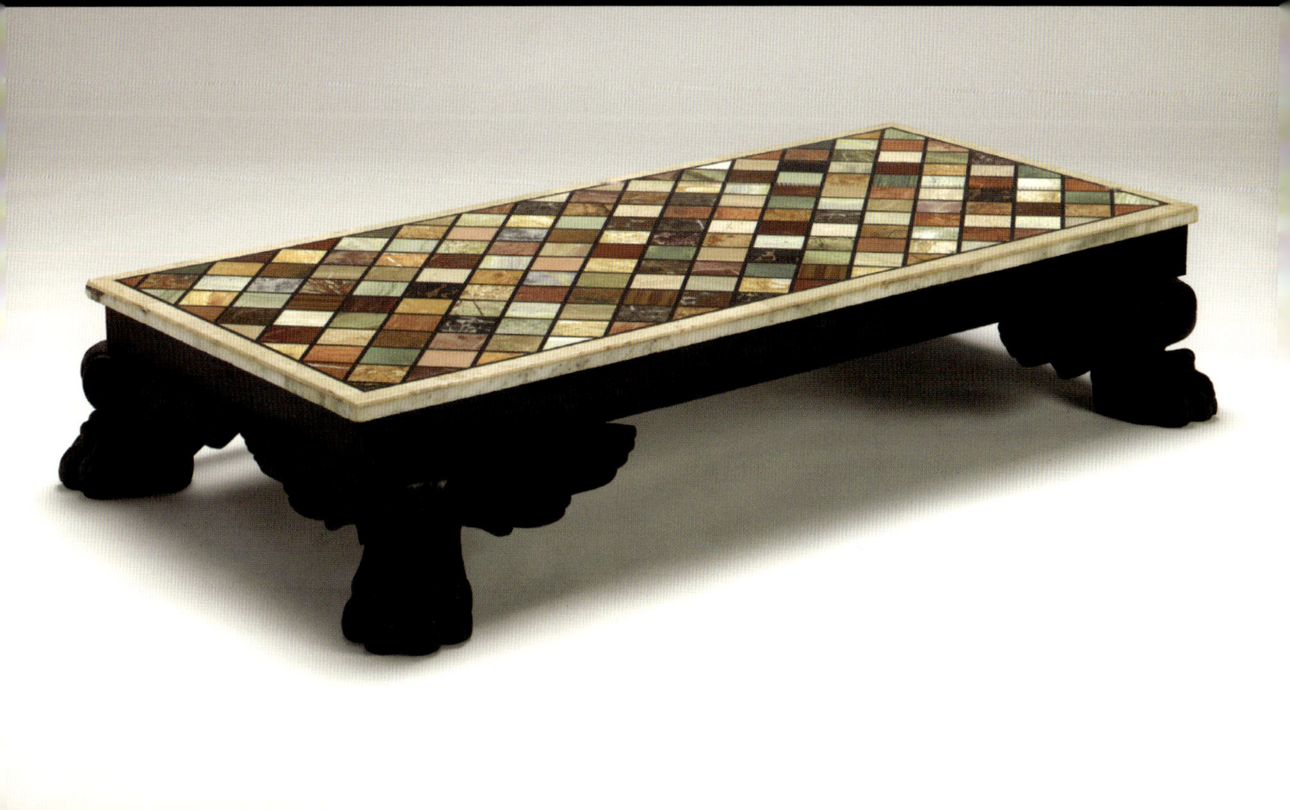

THE FINE
ENGLISH COMPANY

The Fine English Company was conceived by Benedict Wormald after a lifetime of sourcing unique and artisan pieces for himself during his career in the City. Concerned about the decline of traditional skills such as gun making, tailoring and shoe making, and passionate about conserving the values and craftsmanship they inherently represent, The Fine English Company celebrates these timeless traditions in the most visually striking ways. It is the very fact that Benedict doesn't come from a conventional interiors background that brings such color and interest to the creations he offers. His solutions and creativity stem from a genuine love of traditional country pursuits such as polo, shooting, hunting and fishing.

Enhancing this unique set of characteristics, The Fine English Company also showcases the crème de la crème of British craftsmen and their bespoke creations. Specialising in stunning handmade pieces such as upholstered Chesterfields, show-stopping acid hued sofas, zebra skin lined trunks and museum piece beds carved from the highest quality mahogany. Luxury materials like gold, silver, precious and semi-precious stones, classic styles that wouldn't be out of place in a stately home or an Evelyn Waugh novel and meticulous attention to detail are par for the course in every aspect of the work created.

Talent and innovative techniques come alive and stand out, be it in the smallest piece of jewellery or the full interior of a grand stately home. No matter what your taste or your chosen piece, you will receive the most comprehensive and personal service from beginning to end.

All photos courtesy of Rupert Marlow.

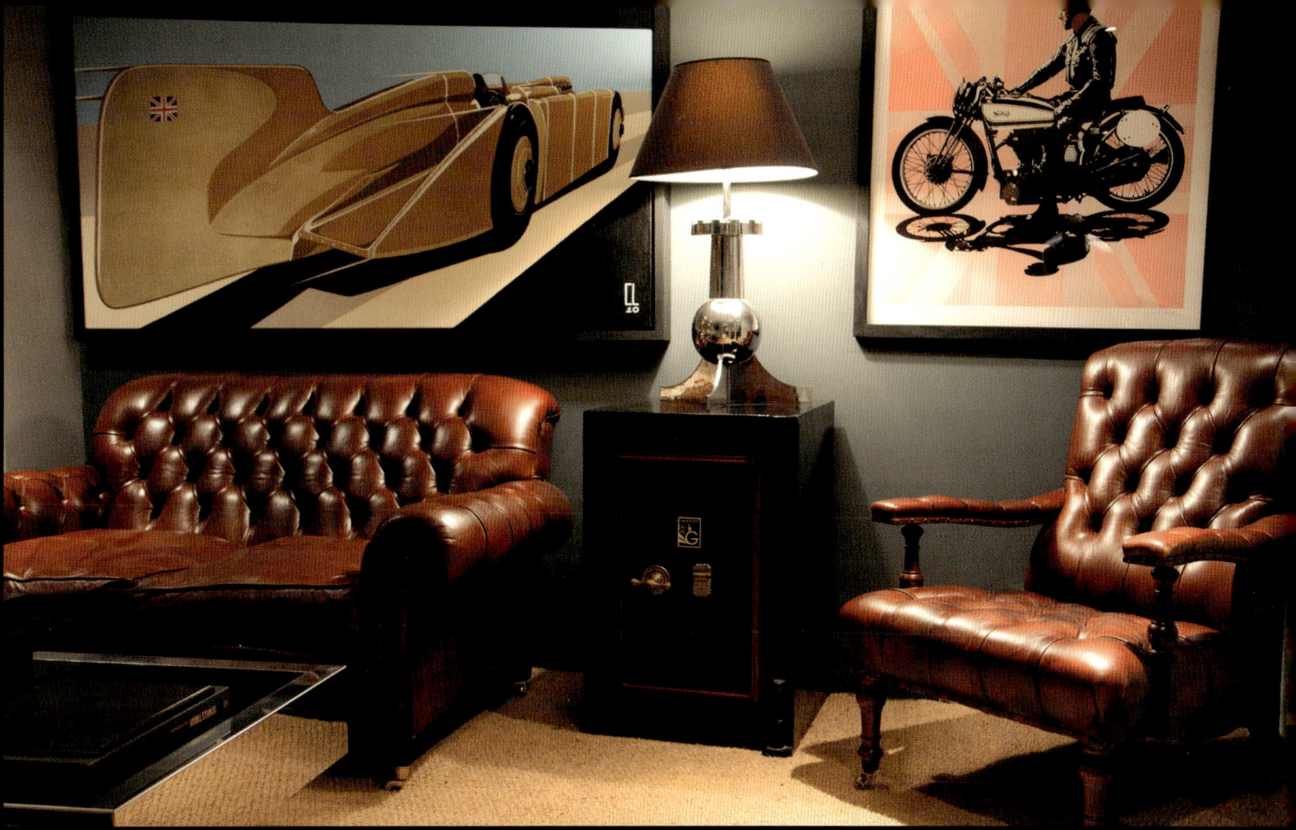

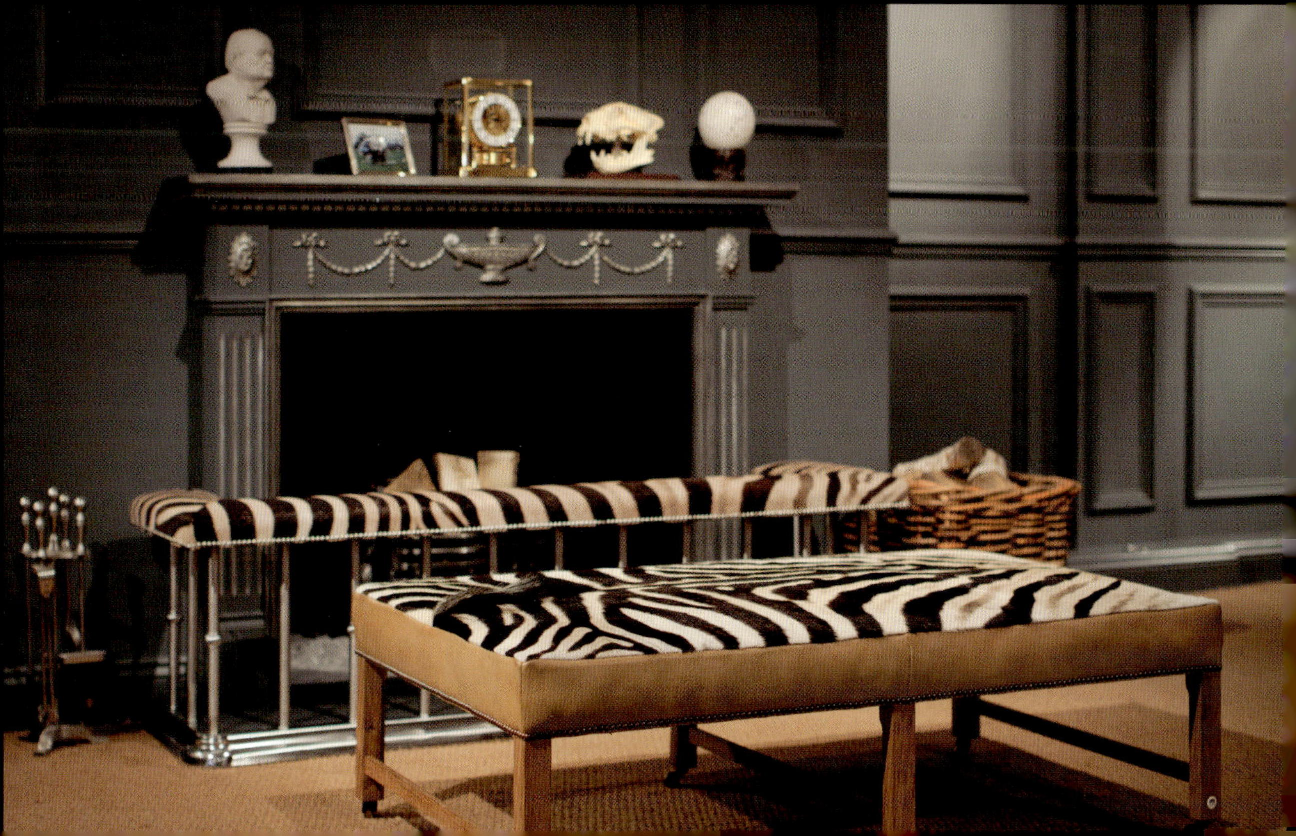

FOLDE

Folde Design Ltd lives by its mantra 'Outstanding interior design, individually yours'. Not only does this dynamic company specialise in innovative interior design and project management, it is also committed to giving its clients an exceptional level of customer service. No project is too complex: Folde can deliver on complete turnkey projects through to specific commissions for interior design, working alongside the client to fulfil their exact requirements from start to finish.

Folde's expertise has evolved over three decades and the company continually develops its capabilities. Being a people business, it benefits from having an excellent team of in-house professionals, and has forged partnerships with some of the best bespoke craftsmen in the industry. Their approach is interactive and based on the fundamental belief that spending time with clients to develop a concept right through

to its entire completion is crucial for success. Once the concept is signed-off, Folde will then apply its professional procurement and project management expertise to ensure that every detail is effectively dealt with; whilst maintaining a critical eye on value for money. There is a wide range of services from navigating the process of obtaining landlord's and statutory permissions, to creating layouts and interior designs, colour consultancy, lighting, audio visual and house management systems for living spaces. Folde ensures that all these elements complement each other and really delivers a unique experience for the client.

Architects, engineers and a wealth of construction specialists are consulted and each project is required to meet exceptional standards of quality from foundations to finishes. Folde's ethos is to assure quality in everything, even those things that the eyes cannot see!

So if you are thinking of transforming any aspect of your living space, Folde Design has the expertise to help you realise your dream.

FORMS
AT FORMWORK

'Philip Michael Wolfson has joined forces with architects Jeremy Peacock and Kasia Piotrowska to create FORMS. This company is devoted solely to creating elegant and inspiring architecture, interiors and furnishings that incorporate the best in planning and design. Internationally acclaimed for a visionary brand of provocative and poetic designs, FORMS integrates striking compositions, cutting edge technology, and innovative materials. As a collaborative of international minds, projects include private residences of national and international significance to the details of the smallest bespoke piece of furniture.

ARCHITECTURE:
Each project embodies the spirit and character of bespoke creation. From the initial client consultation through to completion, there is a strong dialogue between architect, client and consultants. The company seamlessly integrates timeless aesthetic principle whilst working to client's budgets and artistic requirements. FORMS cover every aspect of creating a home, from a new proposal, to renovating and adding onto an existing residence or to historical restoration. Each client plays a crucial part throughout the whole meticulous process making well informed decisions on the design, schedule, and budget.

INTERIORS:
FORMS have a long and distinguished history of work with fine craftsmen and an exceptional understanding of materials. With strong links to some of the finest specialists in America and Europe, creations incorporate leatherwork, stone carving, gilding, lacquer work, glass work, joinery, cabinet making and wood carving. Integrating today's complex infrastructures, and incorporating state of the art technology and exemplary construction with a level of ease and comfort for the client, are primary aspects of a successful project. This ongoing coordination between all parties involved, designers, engineers, consultants and various specialists, allows for the assurance and confidence that the owner's requirements are being met throughout the work.

FURNISHINGS:
Bespoke furniture and built in units are part of the interior design process and FORMS aims to set new standard in their projects. Through the use of the highest caliber materials and overall quality of design and workmanship, the individual pieces designed for each project offer a lifetime investment in creating a legacy and cultural heritage.

Additionally, the firm maintains relationships with associate architectural, engineering and construction firms throughout the world for collaborative team efforts.

FROMENTAL

Design and client services are based at their London head office, with a team of highly talented artists and embroiderers producing the papers from studios in China. Having worked in fashion and interiors, directors Tim Butcher and Lizzie Deshayes have nearly twenty years experience in designing, producing and restoring hand – made wallpapers. Combining the highest levels of workmanship with luxurious fabrics, their distinctly British style blends classicism with the cutting – edge cool of London's fashion scene.

Collections comprise their unique take on Chinoiserie, bold and elegant 20th Century designs as well as subtle, textured Roomskins. Fromental also produce contract and custom work. Production is personally supervised by the directors and each project takes 3 – 4 months on average from idea to delivery.

Fromental continually develop new processes and patterns to create innovative and stylish wallpapers, updating historic motifs with brightness and a dash of wit. Their designs now grace the walls of some of the most prestigious commercial and residential properties around the world including Steve Wynn's resorts in Las Vegas and Macau, China Tang at the Dorchester Hotel, The London NYC and The London LA hotels and The Goring.

Fromental are pioneers in embellishing wallpaper with fine silk embroidery, taking a decorative form to new heights of luxury. The wallpapers are hand – painted prior to being fully or part – embroidered with very fine silk thread available in hundreds of colours. Artists spend up to 600 hours elegantly stitching individual panels.

Fromental's now – signature modern take on 18th Century Chinoiserie utilizing both monochromatic and vibrant colourways has paved the way in reviving the genre.

"The tradition of skilled craft has almost disappeared in Europe so we've chosen to locate manufacturing in the country that hosts the world's best painters and embroiderers for the designs we want to achieve. We have a window in history to produce works of the beauty and skill which have not been witnessed since the 18th Century." Tim Butcher, Creative Director.

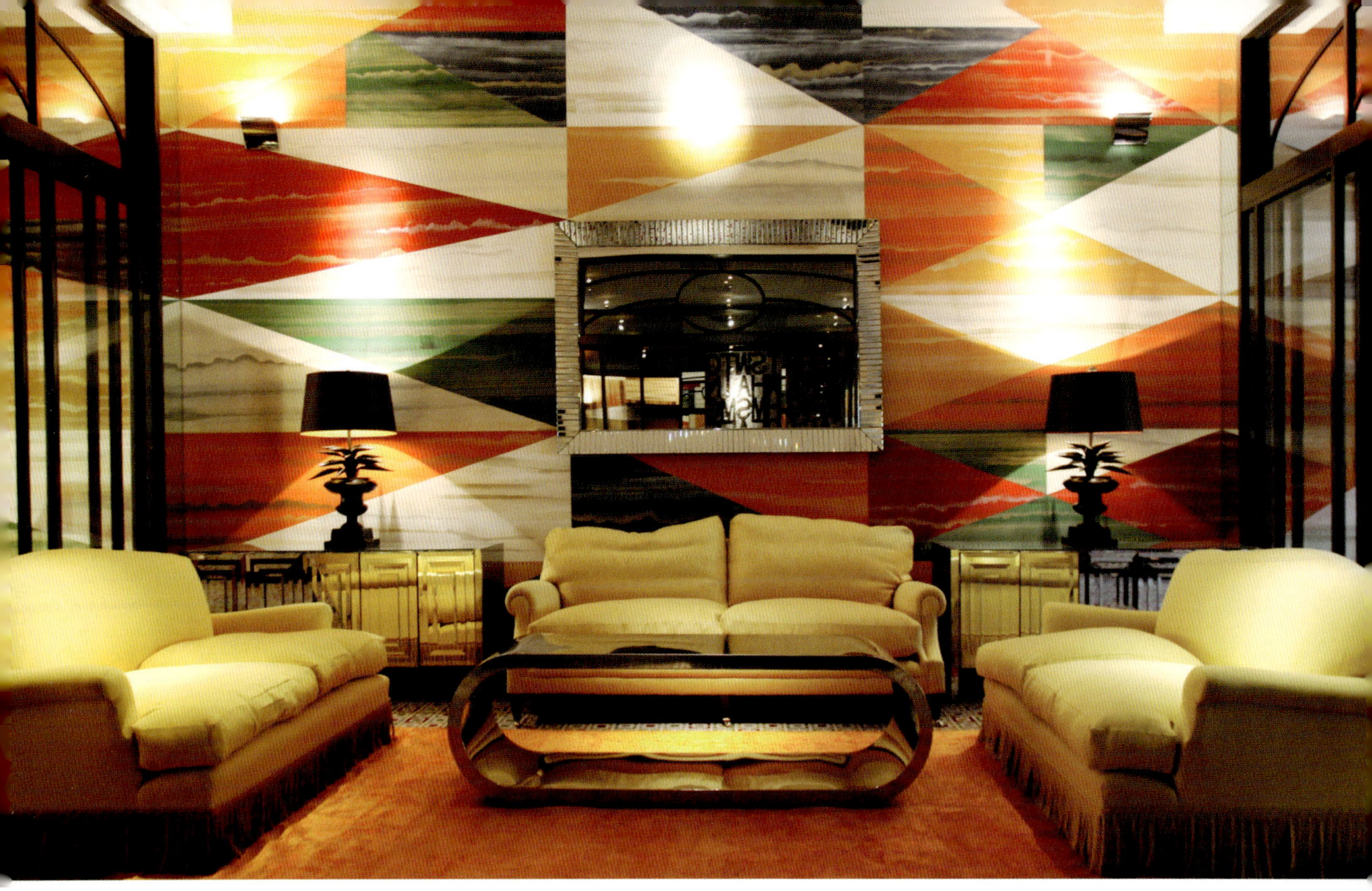

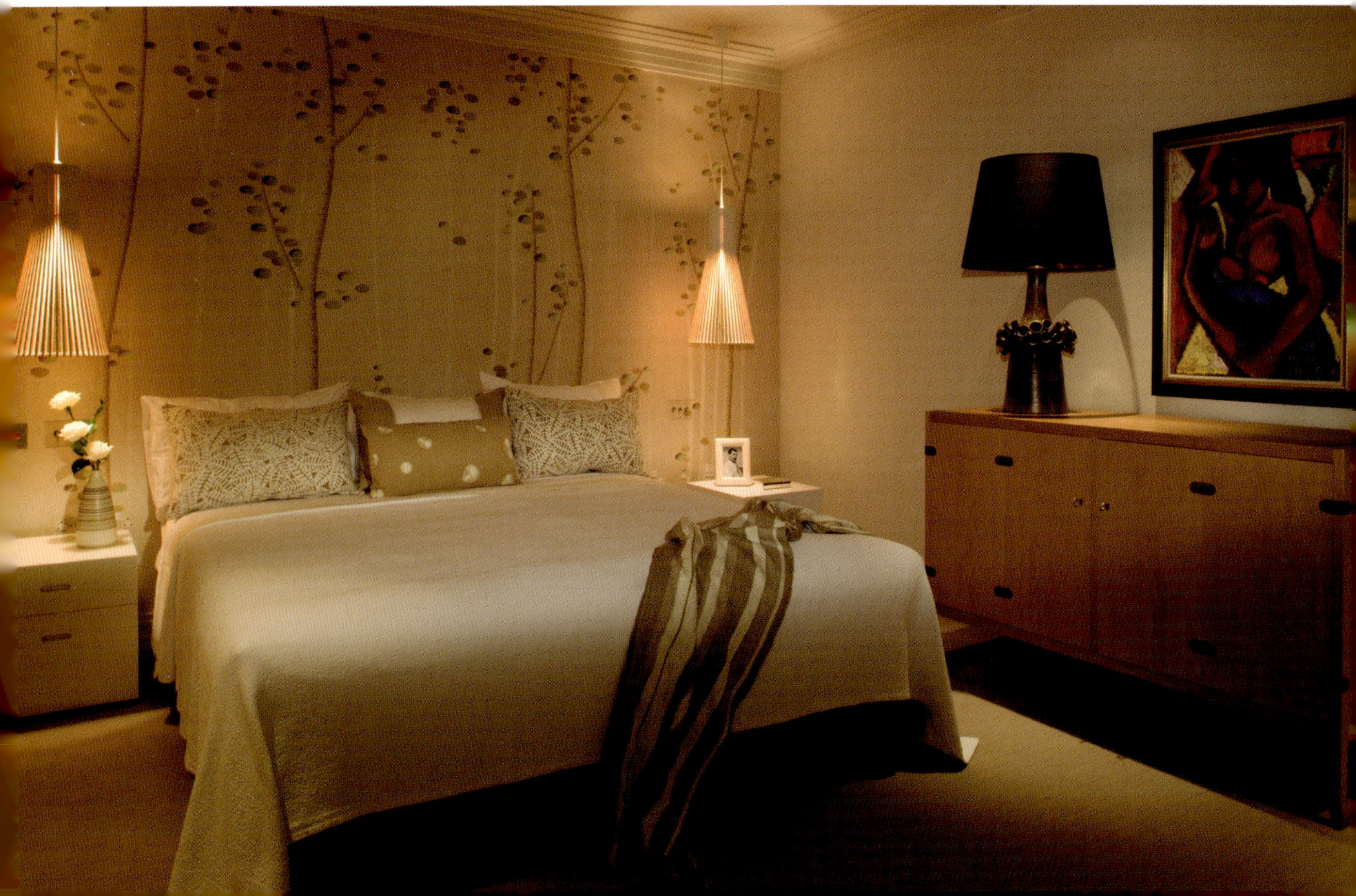

Fromental's design direction is derived from two different angles. Tim, from a maker's side, enjoys the challenge of how things work, and through that process comes up with innovative new designs. Lizzie trained as a textile designer so takes inspiration from the decorative aspects of nature and surface ornamentation. They often work together on a chosen design and the blend of the two very different approaches combines into results they both find pleasing.

Inspiration for their designs is found in everything and anything that catches their eyes. Sources range from 15th Century Flanders tapestries, the description of an interior in a Colette novel and studying the work of China's most loved artist Qi Baishi to the Left Bank of Paris, the Pacific coast highway and London's V&A museum.

"I find the works of past textile designers such as Lewis Foreman Day (a contemporary of William Morris) a great resource. They were not only gifted designers and consummate craftsmen but also had a vast breadth of knowledge of the decorative arts of other nations and eras. Not many people have such dedication to their craft as they did." Lizzie Deshayes

"I'm particularly fond of the great polymath designers and inventors who turn their creative bent to whatever comes their way. The likes of Gio Ponti designing buildings and coffee machines; Buckminster Fuller rethinking concepts such as the house and car. As well as their works, it's their approach and attitude I admire — looking at any item and not being tied to any set process but instead, looking at new ways of creating it." Tim Butcher

If you crave simplicity and yearn for the luxury of living without distractions, then Gavin Jackson is the architect with that rare sensibility you've been searching for.

Gavin has been creating subtle, poetic spaces for his clients at home, work or play for over 20 years. These spaces are designed to work beyond their mere functionality to emanate peace, serenity and calm, providing a haven from the noise and haste of everyday life.

Passionate about these qualities Gavin achieves them with a delicate balance between life, art and nature. He roots his work in the traditions of the visual arts, maintaining a strong relationship with contemporary art as a counterpoint to his focus on nature. Composing buildings with simple forms, planes and lines while opening up internal vistas and editing external views, Gavin then carefully balances natural and artificial light to create a sculptural architecture bathed in light.

His techniques may be complex, but the results are blissfully, beautifully simple.

GAVIN JACKSON

GEORGE SMITH FURNITURE & FABRICS

Proudly British, George Smith produces handmade furniture and fabrics of peerless quality for the most exclusive residences, as well as high end hospitality and yacht projects.

The integrity inherent to the design and craftsmanship across all George Smith creations is a reflection of the company's philosophy and is a solid foundation for their glowing reputation in the business. The time honoured manufacturing techniques of the golden era of upholstered furniture are rigorously adhered to, and where improvements in these techniques can be achieved, they are. It is the timeless designs that allow George Smith products to happily exist within a myriad of interior schemes and to avoid being pigeon-holed in any one genre. Assured of the quality, the designer is free to use George Smith pieces as the blank canvas on which to realise their masterpiece by their combination of pieces, fabric, or the application detail.

George Smith are as comfortable producing completely custom - made pieces inspired by their clients' ideas, as they are in making any of their extensive catalogue of classic designs. This enviable flair for bespoke creations has helped elevate them to the top of their industry. Their client list now includes some of the world's most accomplished private individuals as well as being the first choice of leading designers in the luxury residential, hospitality and yacht markets.

GIBSON MUS|C

When it comes to seamlessly integrating top quality home technology into high-end interior design schemes, Gibson Music is the go-to company for savvy interior designers, architects and discerning private clients alike. Established in 1985, Gibson Music has an industry-leading reputation and takes pride in the fact that, whilst many companies have joined the sector, it has remained at the forefront in terms of pioneering innovation and dependability.

Respected in the business as experts in the field, Gibson Music has waded through the complex offerings of technology, confidently providing tried and tested solutions to its clients. As the expectation is for equipment to be as future-ready as possible, Gibson Music is always on top of the latest developments, ready to embrace the new and the improved, offering installations that are current, sophisticated and, above all, straightforward to use.

The age of internet and satellite has created all sorts of possibilities, encouraging the specification of fully functioning 'smart' homes. Multi-room audio, private home cinema, lighting control, door entry, security and climate control are all typical elements of integrated home technology within a luxury property. Gibson Music installs these features discreetly, thereby respecting and complementing the décor. Everything in the luxury home has the capacity to be controlled by a single touch-screen panel, enabling easy access to all the home automation features.

As part of Gibson Music's bespoke service, maintenance contracts complete the experience. In addition to designing and installing custom solutions for residential properties, Gibson Music incorporates its creative and technical expertise with a clear understanding of a diverse group of disciplines including yachts, ski chalets, boutique hotels and spas. 21st Century technology is yours at the touch of a button – anywhere you wish.

GODRICH INTERIORS

At Godrich Interiors discretion, clarity and trust underpin their highly personal design service. Established in 2003, Godrich Interiors has grown to undertake numerous bespoke residential projects across London, the rest of the UK and Europe, and as far as the Caribbean, Hong Kong and India.

Their dedicated client service, thoughtful design and proficient management continue to attract a discerning customer base searching for creative and exciting design solutions. Through sourcing high quality products, many of which are vintage, their designers are able to put a very personal stamp on any project; the client will feel like they have lived in their new home for years thanks to these thoughtful and individual touches.

The Godrich team has a vast amount of experience to call upon and an increasing portfolio of exquisite properties, many of which are listed or have historical significance. Their extensive network of specialist suppliers and craftsmen can design, specify and install bespoke designs for prestigious assignments anywhere in the world.

With no set design approach, Godrich Interiors are able to tailor their wide knowledge of contemporary and traditional styles to suit each client's needs. A strong appreciation of the customer's privacy is their overriding principle and client satisfaction is of the upmost importance; as a result their service is discreet and subtle yet professional and dependable.

Founders and school friends, Ed Godrich and Rupert Hunt, along with their team of designers, provide a service where financial transparency and confidentiality are paramount. Rupert Hunt's earlier career in the City means that financial management of projects has become fundamental to their offering and Ed Godrich's diverse knowledge of the interiors markets is unmatched.

GOSLING

Grandeur, permanence and a certain classic style characterize Tim Gosling's distinctive, dramatic bespoke furniture and interior designs. Opulent and elegant, Tim's work has graced yachts, country homes, city apartments and corporate boardrooms. The versatility of his style relies on his dedication to tailoring a room and its elements to meet each client's individual tastes and needs. Unusually for a designer at this stage in their careers, Tim prides himself on his personal involvement with every aspect of a project.

Tim graduated from the Central School of Art & Design in 1987 with a BA (Hons.) degree in Theatre Design. His work in theatre included creating set and stage scenes for major West End productions such as Miss Saigon and Starlight Express. He even worked as a set designer for spectacular Las Vegas shows, developing a flamboyant touch that can still be seen echoed in his work today.

In the late 1980's Tim joined David Linley, becoming a director in 1993. At Linley he was influential in developing the company's design style and expanding their bespoke business over 18 years. In 2005 Tim set up on his own, giving him the freedom to design a wider range of furniture while continuing his working relationships with interior designers worldwide.

Gosling's objective is to create classic bespoke furniture and interior design that has style, longevity and integrity. Commissioning begins with an intimate consultation with the clients. Tim does not have a conventional showroom, instead he has established a full working studio from which his clients may commission their project, where a large selection of wood samples, inlays, and different techniques of furniture design and creation are showcased. Drawing inspiration from a library of architectural books detailing styles from the 15th Century onwards, each piece of furniture is then designed and made to exacting standards using fine materials and traditional cabinet making techniques. The same exacting philosophy is applied to the interiors he undertakes.

In just 5 years Gosling has built up an impressive portfolio with commercial projects including The Goring Hotel, the last privately owned hotel in London, in which he designed cutting edge new bedrooms and the impressive downstairs reception rooms. Current projects now include major commissions in Geneva, Florida, and Bahrain as

INTE**R**IORS WITH ART

For over a decade, the dynamic sibling duo of Shailja Vohora and Sanjay Sharma have been creating diverse and lavish bespoke homes from the ground up. With a keen eye for the client's specific needs, refined by their own multi-domiciled perspectives and experience, this boutique entrepreneurial firm provides unique and personalised solutions to high-end interior refurbishments.

IWA partners with their clients to explore and reflect creative options that are acutely sensitive to their patrons' lifestyles. The clients and IWA jointly embark on a learning journey from conception to completion of their projects. This collaborative approach to the vision, blue print, building and execution ensures each task is delivered expediently and within budget. IWA conducts all aspects of construction, design, project management and accessories in-house, to the highest standards of luxury, discretion, practicality and fulfillment.

In every conversation and task, Shailja and Sanjay convey their passion for traditional and contemporary aestheticism, a deep-rooted understanding and care for their clients and their symbiotic partnership that is at the core of IWA's excellence and success. Shailja's creative background and credentials include Inchbald School of Design, Christie's, Sotheby's and the School of Oriental and African Studies. Beyond her 20 years of interior design experience and expertise, her expansive personal and professional fluency in philosophy, history, culture and arts from all over the world, resonate in every interior. She is at the top of her game in understanding an existing collection or creating a home with artistic authenticity.

By perfect contrast and in complement, Sanjay is the business, logistics, project management and precision guru for each assignment. Hailing from the prestigious Carnegie Mellon University followed by

senior leadership positions in business management and consulting, Sanjay renounced corporate America and UK's blue chip corporations to devote his energies to IWA. He masterminds the supply chain, inventory, detailed planning, seamless delivery and round the clock execution. This impressive pair put people first with inordinate elegance, exuberance and humility.

Whether a nursery, a commercial office, London penthouse or a Middle Eastern palace, IWA's hallmark is one of delivering artistic and pragmatic exclusivity. Such is the strength of their clients' testimonials IWA is sought out repeatedly and globally for continued involvement and evolution of their contemporary abodes.

For further information and requests please find all contact details in the index pages 172-175

ISABELLA WOLFE

The distinctive furniture designs of Isabella Wolfe infuse their space with what can only be described as a touch of magic. The look is unusual, unique, curious and captivating with materials that are often rich, sensual and unexpected.

Launched exclusively at Los Angeles Niche showroom in May 2010, the press has already picked up on Isabella Wolfe's sensational appeal, showcasing the range online in Vogue.com and in both the Sunday Times and Livingetc magazines in the UK.

Founded by Nicole Fuller, a prestigious interior designer who has twice been nominated for the Andrew Martin Designer of the Year Award and has designed such acclaimed interiors as the historical Stanhope Hotel, NY, the name of the firm was chosen to commemorate the famed designer Elsie de Wolfe, one of Nicole's personal inspirations. Fuller's wider inspiration for Isabella Wolfe is the elegance and sophistication of European furnishings in the 18th and 19th centuries combined with a fun-loving sense of style, curiosity and love of the new.

The wide spectrum of furniture, accessories and bespoke designs that the design firm creates are signed and numbered limited editions that bring that special, indefinable something to any interior.

For further information and requests please find all contact details in the index pages 172-175

LIVING IN SPACE

When Living in Space appeared on the scene with their pioneering approach to environmentally - friendly living, people sat up and took notice. Before this there had been stylish, unusual and innovative interior designers and architects, but few who had offered such a comprehensive and intelligent range of services as Living in Space. More than ten years have passed since their beginnings and their portfolio of clients has steadily flourished. Clients will entrust the company with the conceptual design of their living space right through to its actual build, including tailor-made furniture and soft furnishing. The difference however lies with the company's fundamental passion for the environment and a sense that responsible living should be luxurious, chic and part of our psyche. Thanks to the perfect synergy of exceptional design quality and the environmentally-friendly use of materials, the organic home has become a tenable and attractive reality.

No project is too small or too big, no detail too trivial or too complex for the skilled team at Living in Space. In-house architects, project managers, spatial and interiors designers and soft furnishings experts work their magic to create the ultimate haven of peace. So if the notion of refurbishing your home whilst protecting the environment seems inconceivable, think again. Living in Space will take the pain out of every process with astonishing ease and elegance. So all you have to do is sit back and enjoy your finished living space and marvel as it 'works' for you.

LIVING IN SPACE ECOHOUSE

Combining luxury with environmentally friendly living

Living In Space have always been a forward thinking company and with climate change now a serious issue on the world agenda, they aim to show people how living a life of luxury can be done in a way that does not harm the environment.

Whether building from scratch or refurbishing an existing property, there are numerous ways in which you can reduce your carbon footprint and also save yourself money. Furthermore, these talented designers are passionate about spreading the message that living in an environmentally friendly way actually adds to the comfort and luxury of a home. Measures like reinforced insulation and efficiently managed heating systems allow for a greater depth of comfort. Never too hot, never too cold - there is a perfectly balanced temperature regulation that can be set differently for each room to suit your needs.

There is also something very satisfying about actively generating your own energy and therefore not being subject to rising energy prices. With recent government incentives and technology improving all the time, it now makes commercial sense to invest in renewable energies within the home. Living in Space work with their clients to present all the options available to them and ensure that the right products are specified for use in their home.

The 'Ecohouse' concept allows people to witness the working success of certain eco measures in their own home while also enhancing their standard of living.

1) Triple glazed windows with low emissivity coatings and gas.
2) Fireplace fuelled by bio ethanol, a renewable substance produced from agricultural bi-products that gives off no smoke or harmful emissions.
3) Ecostone flooring manufactured using natural materials, 70% of these materials are reprocessed using environmentally friendly methods.
4) Kitchen tops manufactured from recycled materials such as mirror, glass, porcelain, vitrified ash and earthenware.
5) FSC certified wooden floors.
6) Aerated taps, dual flush toilets and shower flow limiters.
7) Green wall

8) Super insulated walls
9) Photovoltaic panels
10) Solar thermal collectors
11) Rain water harvesting system
12) Ground source heat pump
13) General: VOC free wall paints and eco wall paper made from sustainably managed forests, LED/ low energy throughout, furniture sourced and made sustainably, LED television, A+ rated appliances. Intelligent mechanical and electrical systems that manage all the heating, lighting, security etc in the most energy efficient way.

LORCA DESIGN BY
ELENA KARAMAN KARIĆ

Elena Karaman Karić founded LORCA DESIGN to unite two of her passions: art and design. The company offers flawlessly designed bespoke furniture as well as luxury interior design services. Elena Karaman Karić was born into an arts - oriented family in Belgrade and developed a fascination for the arts from an early age. She draws her design inspiration from her extensive travels around the world. Elena credits her multi-ethnic heritage (her grandmother is Peruvian) as the key contributing factor in her creative vision today.

After studying interior design and psychology, Elena's path to furniture design began gradually; initially redecorating apartments, then large residences and office spaces. The various challenges that she faced while working on all these projects provided her with the perfect platform to exhibit her talent for combining luxurious design and functionality. As her company grew, so did her need to express herself in more than just interior design and the perfect opportunity arose when she couldn't find the right furniture to complete her vision of the space. She designed a few bespoke furniture pieces for her client at the time in order to complete the job but the reactions were enough to persuade her to venture into a new area of design.

Sometime after, her first limited collection of unique furniture pieces was presented to her clients and colleagues. The secret behind the success of her bespoke furniture design is the fusion of cutting-edge techniques with Elena's artistic vision to craft the perfect piece of furniture for every client. The aim is to blend furniture design with the overall ambience thus maximizing the qualities of each space. Throughout her ten year interior design career, Elena has worked precision, passion and creativity into her exclusive design work, incorporating classic elements as well as innovative ideas to fulfill client's needs. Her signature pieces include handmade doors, beds, dressers and chests and she collaborates with artists, sculptors and floral designers to transform her vision from dream to the reality she has always envisaged.

LORCA DESIGN opened its first showroom in Belgrade last autumn and received accolades from industry experts and clients alike. The London showroom is planned for opening at the beginning of 2012.

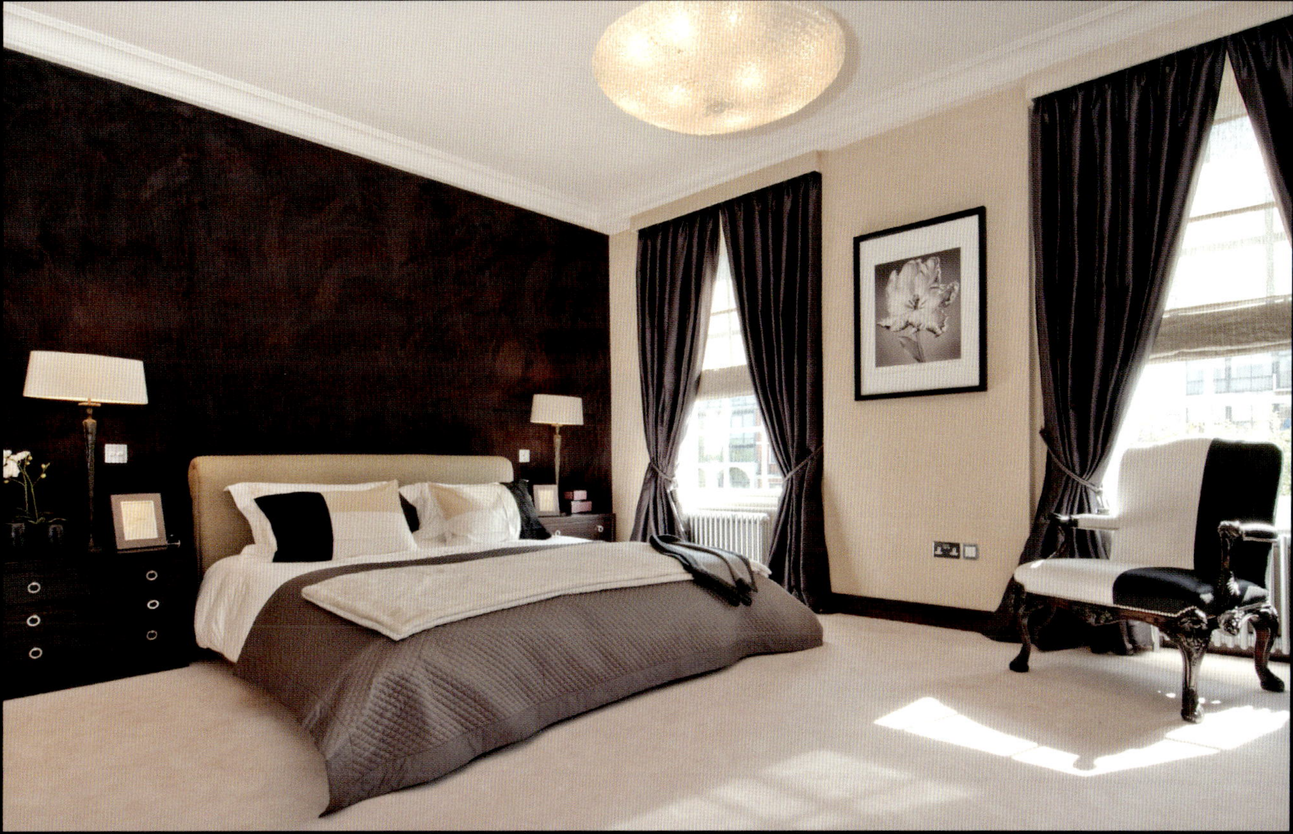

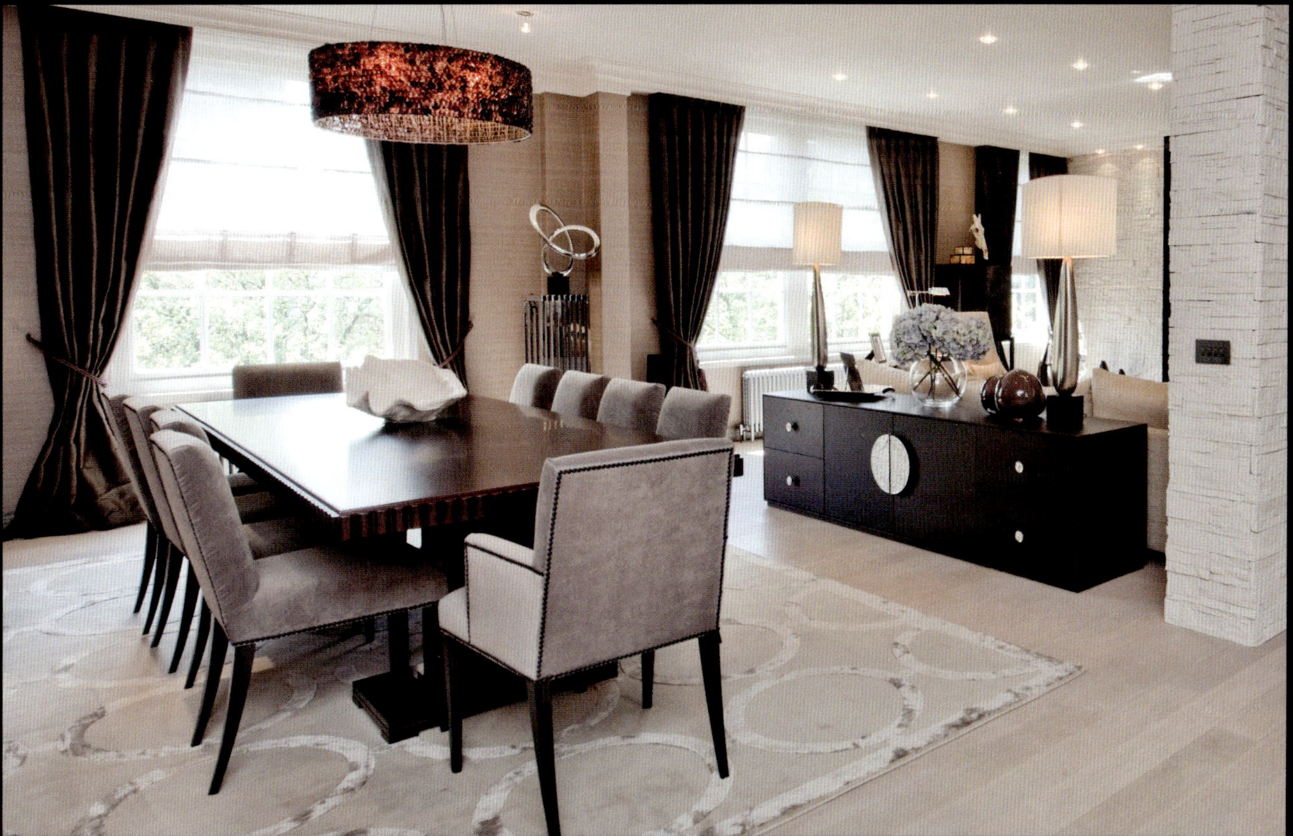

NUTTALL

Nuttall is the shared vision of two sisters, Gytha Bouchon and Amber Aikens, whose aim was to create a collection of furniture and home accessories that represented "the accumulation of small details done to perfection". Taking a tour of their showroom in Chelsea Green's Pond Place, it seems their dream has been realised.

The range of colourfully – upholstered ottomans, footstools, sofas, club chairs and accessories are designed with a charmingly English flair and made according to exacting standards of the best European craftsmanship. Each piece is made to order and delivered with a certificate of authenticity. (The opulent Loro Piana Interiors range is also on hand for a sumptuously tactile finishing touch.) Scrunitising the items on display, each piece is clearly made to last.

Gytha, Creative Director of the brand says, "our vision for Nuttall is to produce beautifully made pieces that will, with love and care, last for generations. Each detail is meticulously thought through, using the finest raw materials and the very best craftsmanship. In decades to come, if someone were to strip back a Nuttall sofa for re – upholstering, I'd like to know that the person would admire the sturdiness of the frame and notice how much care was taken in making it."

Both Gytha and Amber have backgrounds that shape the high standards and creativity of their business. Gytha's Furniture and Fine Arts Diploma from Sotheby's was followed by her graduation from the prestigious Inchbald School of Design. Three years of working under Sally Metcalfe at George Spencer Designs prepared her to launch her own award – winning venture, Gytha Nuttall Designs, in 2000. Amber has worked with Michel Bourdin, Marco Pierre White, Dorla Loewenstein, Mark Birley and Robert Earl, developing her intimate knowledge of the world of business and luxury. But her love of beauty and craftsmanship was founded long before her adult career took off.

"As children we were taken to live all over the world by our parents, from New York and Switzerland to the Bahamas and the South of France," says Amber. "This has given us, and by extension our collection, a cosmopolitan outlook with a dash of English eccentricity. We are looking to grow and develop Nuttall into a complete lifestyle brand over the next few years, to include everything you might need for your home – from candles and paint, to beds and linen." So watch this space.

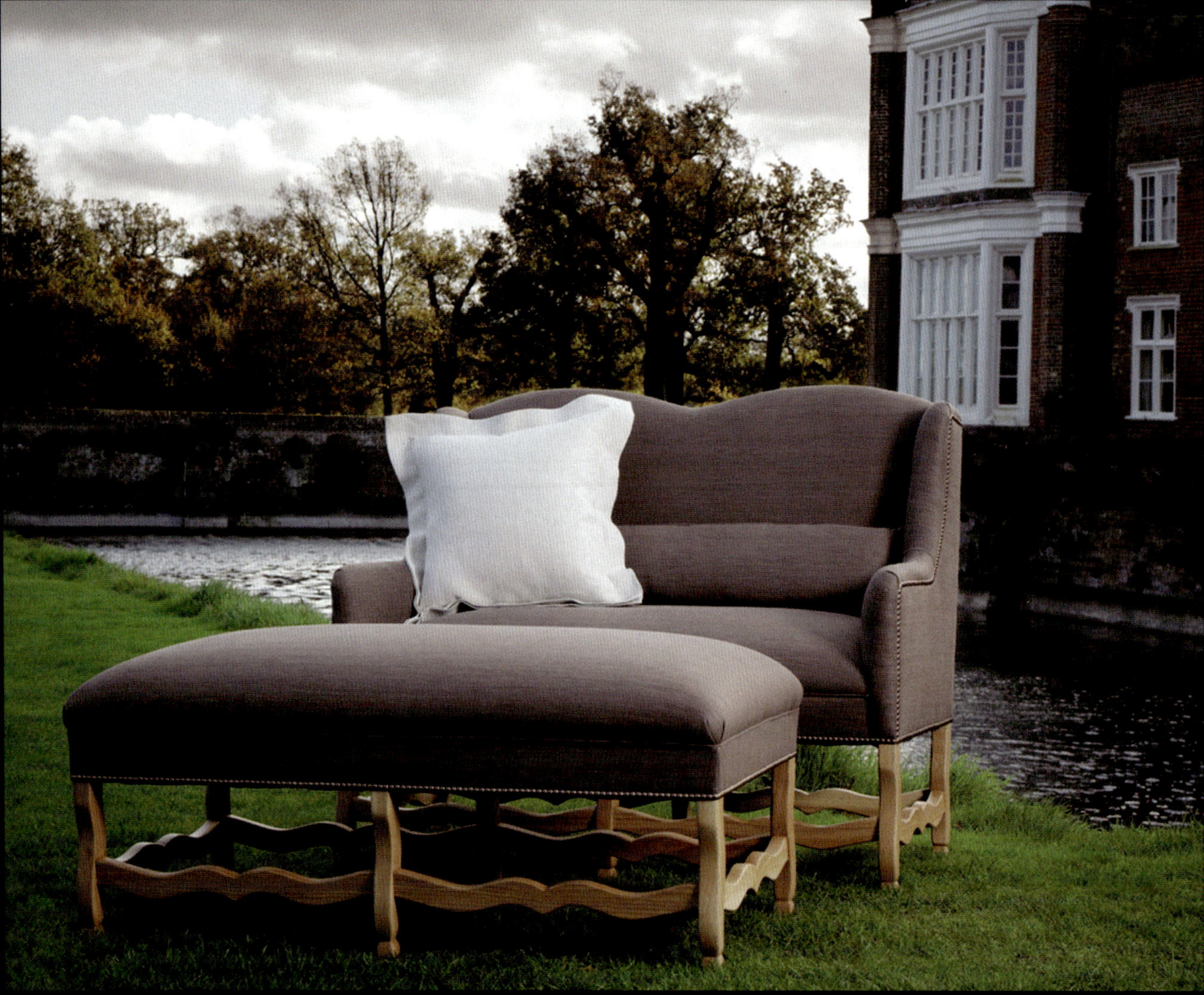

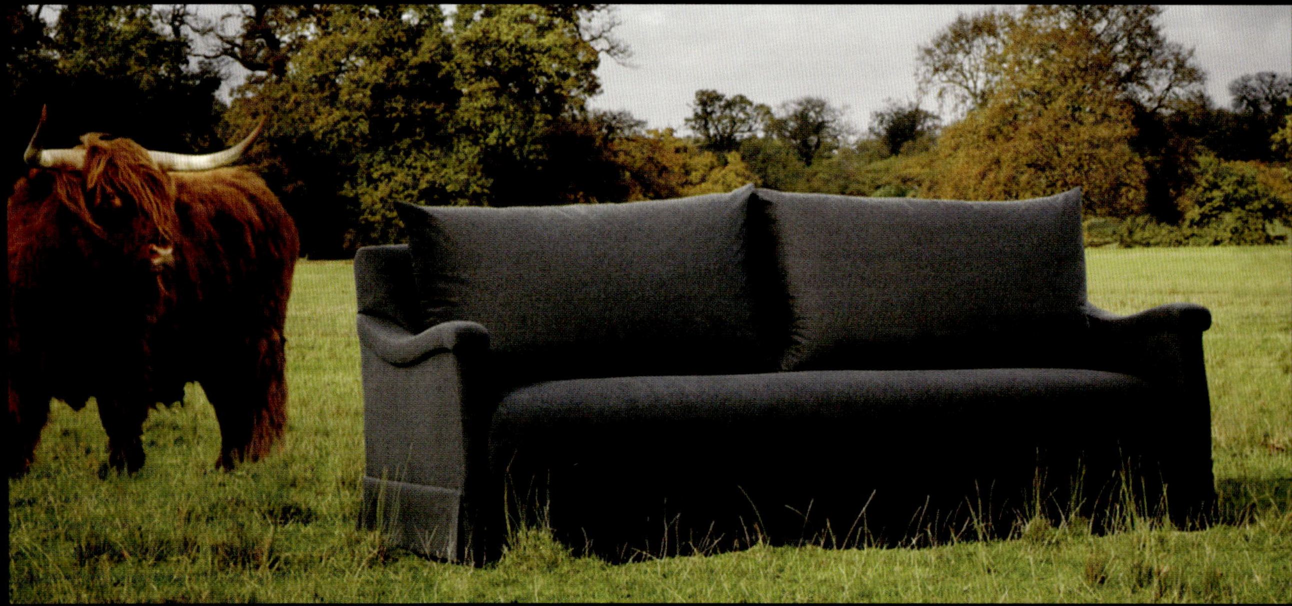

"From historic conversions on an ambitious scale, to luxury modern design, R Interiors are hard to beat" Occasionally outrageous, often quirky and at all times interesting, their specially tailored solutions breathe fresh air into an excitingly diverse range of properties – from casinos and bars, luxury hotels and office spaces to high-end residential in classical and contemporary spaces. As such, their portfolio of work is fantastically varied, pushing the boundaries of architecture and interior design through the use of bespoke materials, space planning, furnishings and finishes. The team expertly transforms tired, outdated spaces into seriously hot properties that are invariably the talk of the town.

Essentially, R Interiors pride themselves not only on the ultimate success of these spaces, but also on the relationships that they strive to nurture with their clients. Rachel explains, "How we start a project is just as important to us as how we finish it. Interior design is more than just a process. It should be enjoyed from the initial meeting right through to project completion, as it is a creative collaboration - it can be described almost as a journey that has to be shared with your client from start to finish. For us this begins with finding a common language that creates a clear, understandable dialogue. An ability to listen to and understand each client from the outset sits at the very core of our approach."

This passion for creativity and collaboration culminates in beautifully considered spaces that boast texture, depth, integrity and style. R Interiors have an enviable ability to achieve remarkable commercial and living environments realized to the highest standards, a talent that allows them to walk away from projects believing that, as they say, "the bench is well and truly marked."

"The experience with R Interiors was intoxicating. Their energy and enthusiasm in every aspect of the project made for an exceptional affair." Ezra Chapman - Private Client.

R INTERIORS

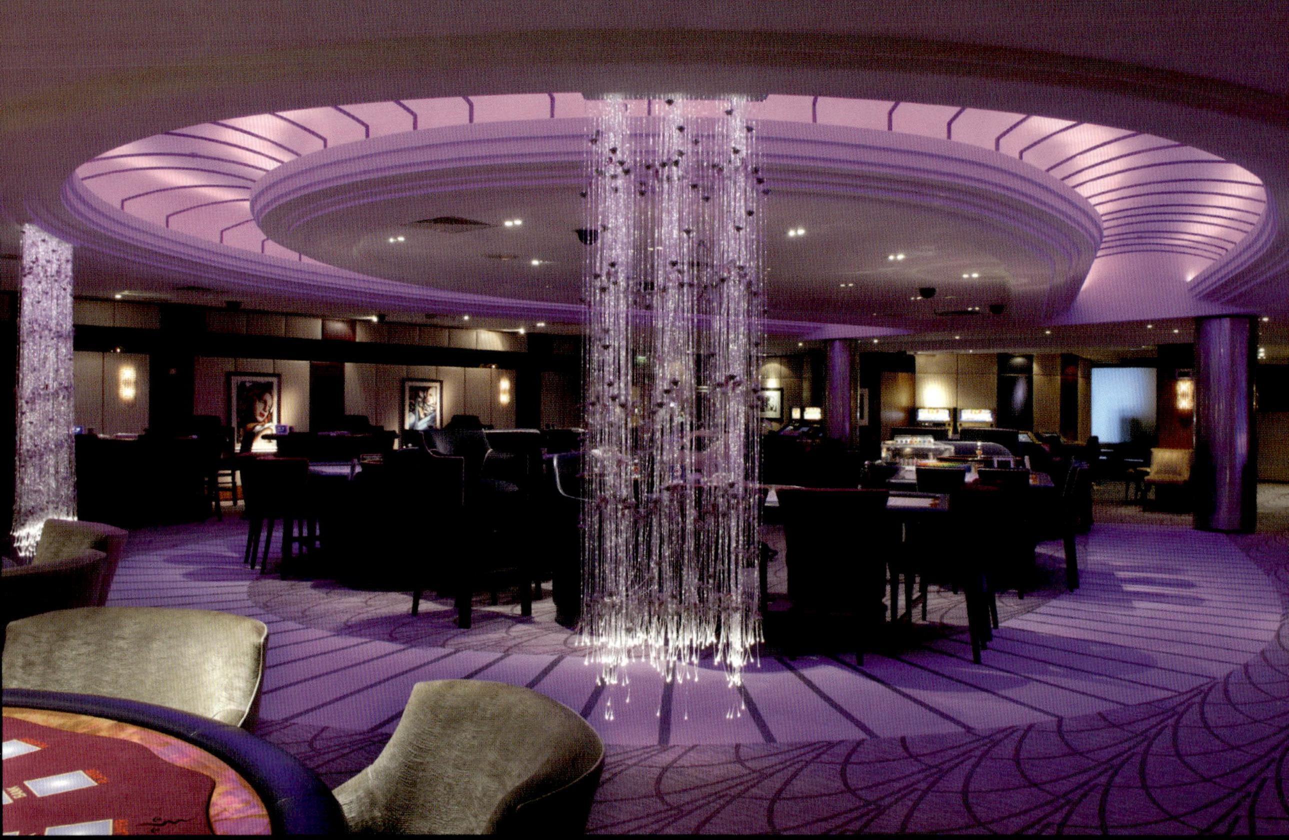

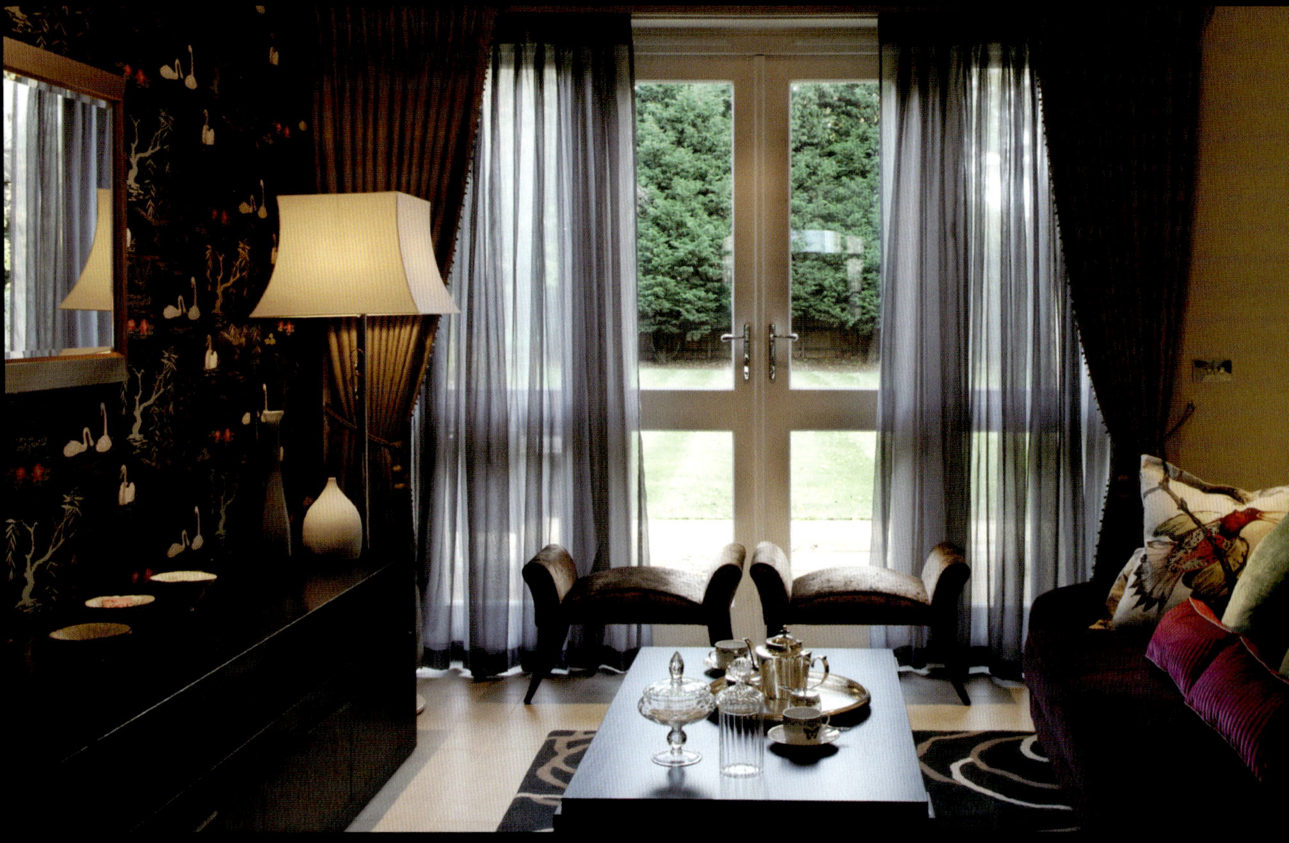

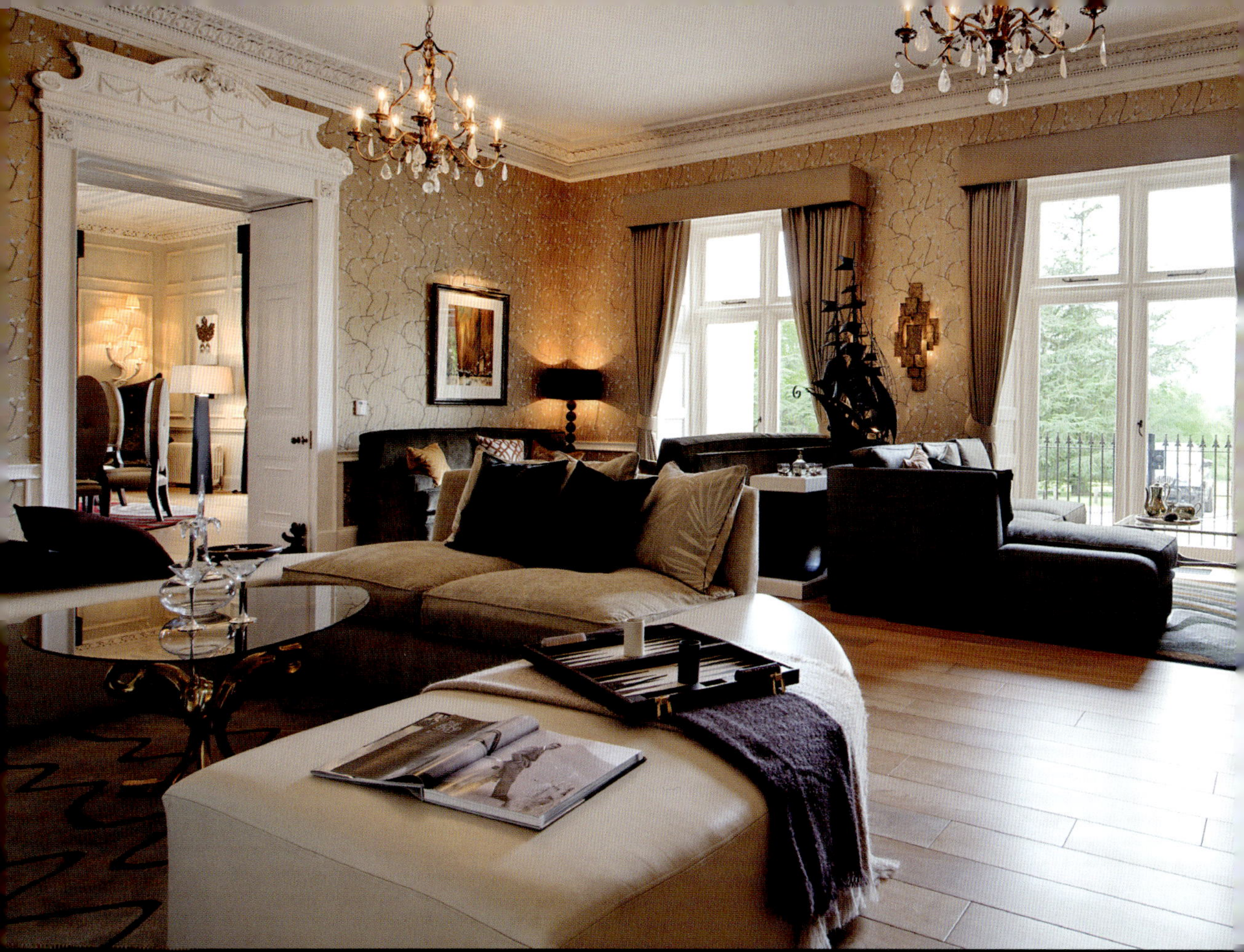

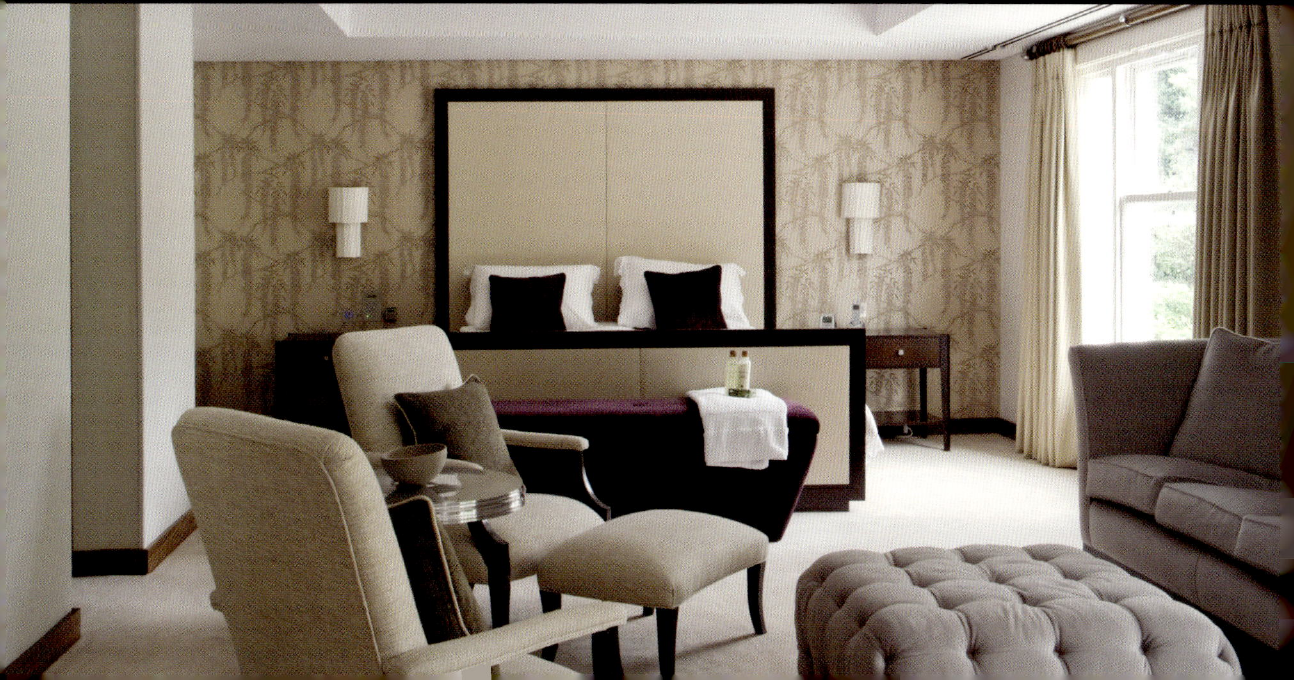

SHARON MARSTON

Pioneering the use of fibre optic technology in bespoke lighting, Sharon Marston's studio has won international acclaim for its range of breathtaking chandeliers, vibrant illuminated backdrops and luxurious room dividers that blur the boundary between sculptural installation and lighting scheme.

Working on an architectural scale Sharon Marston designs are grand and inspiring additions to large corporate spaces, and emphatic, dramatic statement pieces installed in domestic interiors.

The pieces have a signature ethereality, elegance and organic form. Rich, glossy black bone china petals are arranged in waves amongst long strands of light-emitting fibres to create dramatic landscapes in the evocative 'Storm' piece. The Spiral light unfurls with rhythmic grace from its ceiling suspension, and sumptuous, glossy crinolin is gathered into swirls in the opulent 'Ruche' piece. Materials such as fine bone china, hand-blown glass and woven polymers are commissioned for each project to work in harmony with the fibre optic filaments and colours can be selected by the client from a range of hues to create wholly unique, customised pieces.

Since the studio was established in 1997 Sharon has built a team of highly skilled staff who handcraft the decorative components of the lights to the client's exact specifications. The work combines traditional processes and techniques with contemporary design and fuses materials sampled from a range of industries and craft disciplines.

Working with a team of specialist engineers Sharon Marston studio has the ability to produce lights for a range of high-end applications. Projects vary from private residences to large-scale features in the commercial and hospitality sectors worldwide. Each piece is designed and hand crafted in their London based studios and her team work on site, assembling all the decorative components and supervising the installation of the piece to ensure the highest quality of service whatever the scale and wherever the location you choose.

SHELLEY SAFARI

Shelley Safari offers a personal, informal and insightful 'best friend' approach to interior design, with an understanding of the importance of creating a home which reflects the character and individuality of her clients, as well as providing comfort, practicality and the enjoyment of everyday surroundings.

Combining her fresh approach to the interior design service, her experience within major art galleries and auction houses and her ability to source art and unusual objects from around the world, Shelley has created a unique design process which is a pleasant and enjoyable experience and which culminates in a distinctly individual home.

Photography by: Natalie Kadas

SONITE

Over 2,000 years ago master Greek craftsmen elevated mosaics to a true art form by creating highly sophisticated tableaux of inspiring image and colour. You could say that Sonite Surfaces is a product of this artistic tradition. Highly skilled craftsmanship coupled with groundbreaking technological advances have catapulted Sonite's mosaic and wall covering creations into the higher echelons of international design. The company's designs have garnered top industry awards with inspired collections ranging from three-dimensional tiles which emulate the pearlescent nacre of seashells, to highly sophisticated patterns of both organic and geometric origin. In 2009 Sonite received two highly prestigious Good Design awards from Japan for mosaics and for their solid surfacing materials and continued on in 2010 to earn top honours at the "Coverings" international wall-covering tradeshow in the United States. In 2011, Sonite also picked up awards for the best on-trend product with the "3-Layer La Concha" tile at the highly competitive "Surfaces" show in Las Vegas. These prized accolades are a measure of the success and passion with which Sonite has become synonymous with elegant surface coverings innovation.

The Sonite 'S' logo draws its inspiration from the symbol for "infinity" ∞ echoing their infinite and never-ending commitment towards innovation, development and creative expression. The emergence of this logo from the 'I' in SONITE signifies the infinite stream of (I)deas that flow from the company

VIOLET & GEORGE
THE INTERIOR TAILORS

Specialising in beautifully made, cleverly designed soft furnishings inspired by contemporary fashion and architecture, Violet & George is a label set to revolutionise the industry. Their work ranges from traditional made-to-measure curtains, throws, headboards and cushions to unique creations such as window dressings, customised furniture and distinctive tailor-made lampshades. By mixing modern fabrics with vintage trimmings and bringing back traditional techniques such as smocking and pleating, Violet & George move away from recent trends for bland simplicity, reviving the beauty and complexity of the old while bringing depth and interest to the new.

Founder Nicky Mudie explains that techniques such as bespoke lampshade-making have become something of a dying art. Modern manufacturing techniques, changing fashions and mass overseas imports have stifled these once workaday skills and rendered them almost obsolete. Violet & George seek to redress this balance by rejuvenating the art of elaborately hand-pleated, tucked, smocked, gathered and stretched designs. They can make lampshades to any practical shape and size, offering a fully bespoke service with few restrictions to limit their clients' imaginations. Clients can either supply their own fabrics or Violet & George can suggest choices from a huge catalogue of silks. Trawling vintage fairs for the perfect trimming often gives Violet & George its unique finishing touch.

Violet & George do not specialise in lampshades alone. Nicky's background gives her the knowledge to understand client's needs and to complete their schemes with fabrics, lighting, furniture and accessories from a large samples library housed in Violet & George's Fulham studio. As a designer, her bias is towards creating something unique for her clients, taking a piece of existing furniture and adding interesting details or making curtains with a twist that become an art form in themselves. She is currently working on a range of contemporary lightshades in modern silks that are inspired by a catalogue of Victorian designs.

PHILIP MICHAEL WOLFSON

In the 21st century, architecture aspires to sculpture on a monumental scale and on a different level, experimental furniture design is at the forefront, approaching fine art with just that relative element of function.

Philip Michael Wolfson, the son of a NASA engineer was born in 1958 in Philadelphia, Pennsylvania. He studied architecture at Cornell University, Ithaca, New York and at the Architectural Association, London, England, where he was discovered by Zaha Hadid. After completing his studies he spent the next ten years as head of design with her. In 1991 Wolfson established his own studio and has worked throughout Europe and the USA on residential interiors and functional art pieces shown at leading international art and design exhibitions, galleries, and public venues.

He has established his distinctive pathway, re-examining the forms and ideas of the early 20th century Modernist movements, particularly Constructivism and Futurism. His unique approach to design and art is informed by the dynamics of fracture and fragmentation – layering and manipulating his materials into fluid shapes and forms, where the dynamics of light, shadow and reflection are an integral part of the seduction of the work. They are elegant, graceful designs, easily resembling elongated black swan wings in repose; layered geological contortions, or the energetic movements of an impassioned orchestral conductor.

The exquisite use of noble materials such as woods, glass, metals and stones, as well as new materials, such as carbon fiber, brings dynamic elegance and an individual contemporary feeling that enhances his unique approach.

Works by Philip Michael Wolfson have been shown at, or are included in numerous international collections including the Victoria & Albert Museum (London,UK), the Foundation Cartier (Paris, FR), and the Price Tower Arts Center (Bartlesville, USA). His designs are on display at renowned galleries (Contrasts, Shanghai; Franziska Kessler, Zurich; The Apartment, London; Sebastian + Barquet, New York), at high-profile design art fairs (Art Basel, Design Miami, Salone Internazionale del Mobile, Milan, TEFAF, Maastricht) and at auctions, mainly Phillips de Pury in London and New York.

3 recent books featuring works:

Once Upon a Chair; Die Gestalten Verlag, Berlin 2009
Limited Edition; Birkhauser, Basel 2009
Desire; Die Gestalten Verlag, Berlin 2008

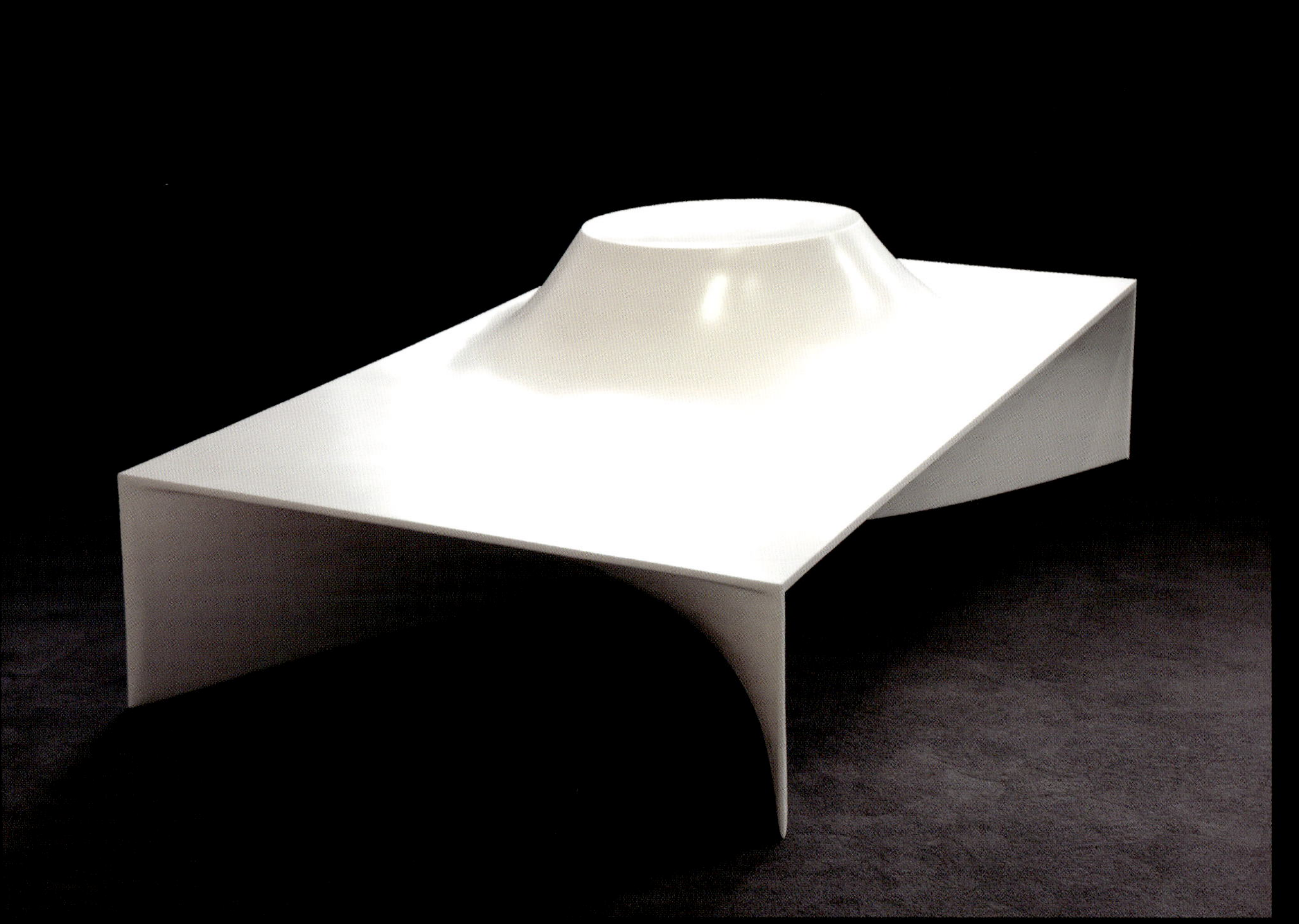

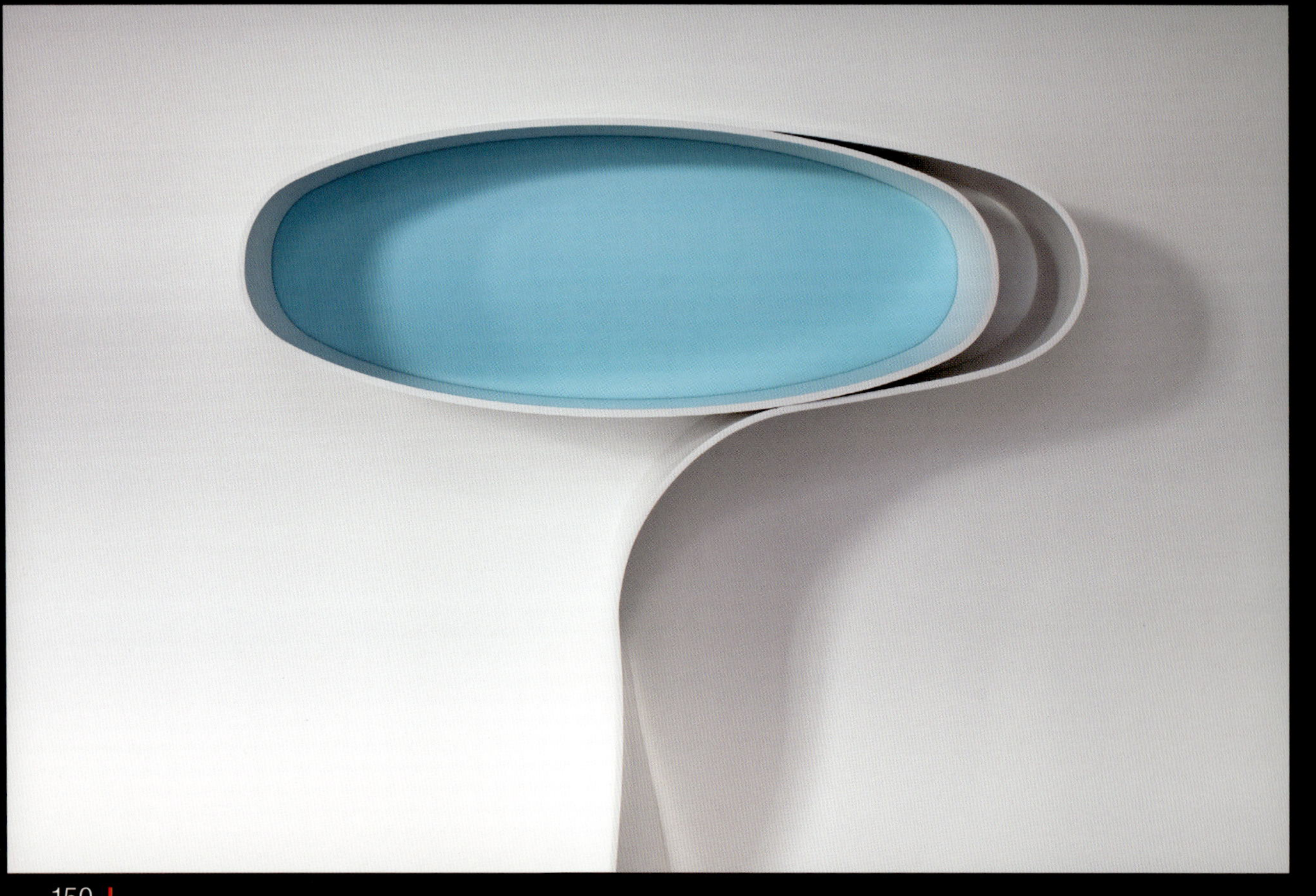

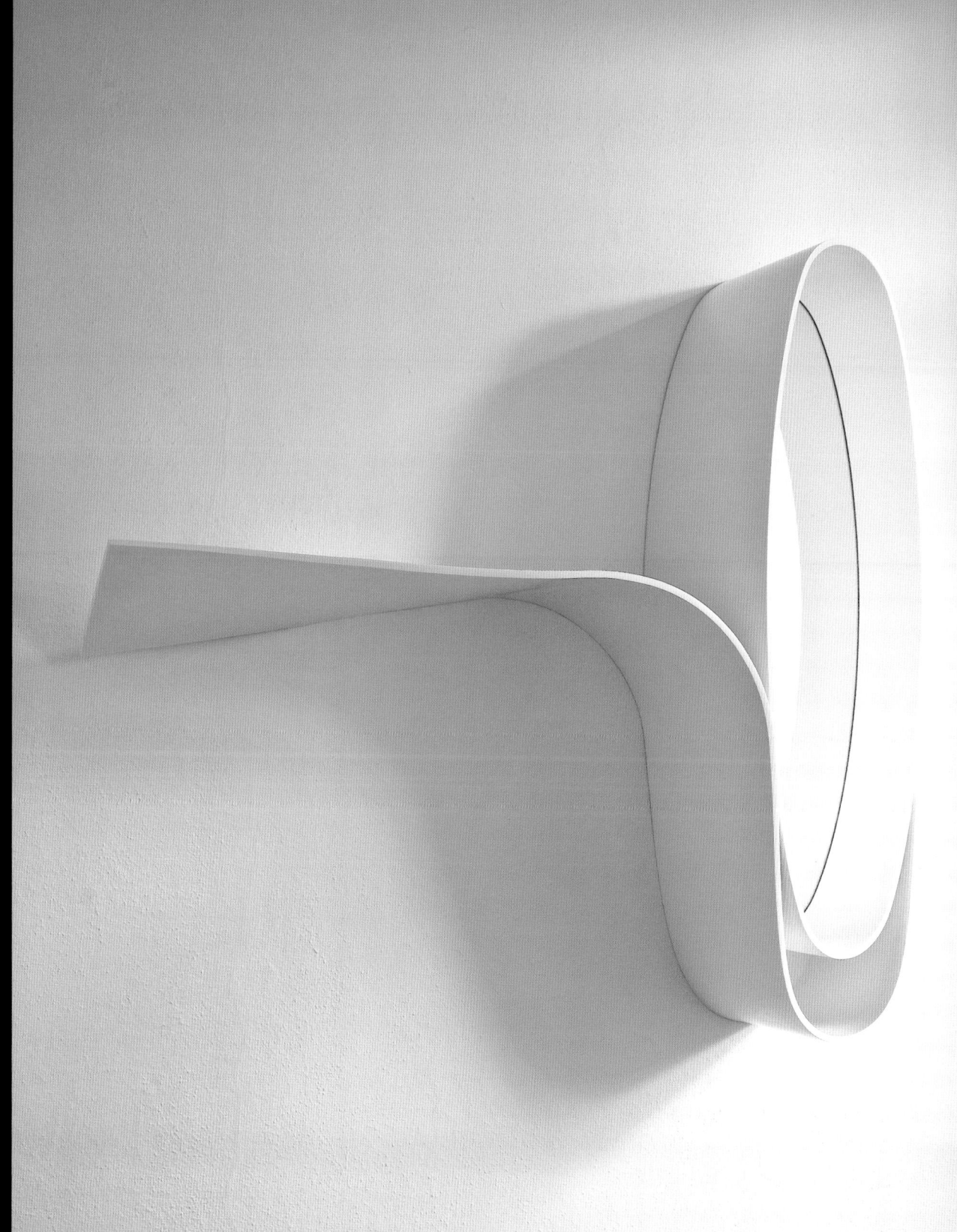

BENJAMIN FRANKLIN HOUSE

Benjamin Franklin's lifestyle in London in the 18th century.

If like most passionate home decoration researchers you have an overwhelming curiosity to catch a glimpse inside the homes of the rich and famous, then here is an unmissable opportunity to learn about the living habits of one of the most influential and inspiring men in history. Benjamin Franklin was a scientist, Enlightenment philosopher, inventor, founding father of the United States of America and pioneer of both electricity and social justice. Very few people realise that Franklin spent a significant portion of his career living in London and 36 Craven Street is the only home of his to survive, now a fully restored and imaginatively curated museum in a fascinating stuccoed terrace house off the Strand in the West End. 36 Craven Street is a beautifully preserved piece of world history, but it's been a long and rocky road to recognition for the property, which remains one of London's best-kept secrets.

The history of 36 Craven Street was very nearly forgotten entirely as the house was left to crumble in the punishing aftermath of the Second World War. A charity set up in the late 1970s acknowledged the building's importance but not much happened until the late 1990s, when initial support from the RSA helped kick-start the conservation effort. Eventually, following complex and expensive restoration and with substantial help from the National Lottery fund, the house was opened to the public in January 2006 marking Franklin's 300th birthday and perfectly illustrating his personal history and the typical 18th Century interior that was its backdrop.

The house itself was built around 1730 and the architecture is a good example of the early Georgian brick faced town houses which were being built all over London in various sizes at this time. Franklin's home was a typical middle class house with two main rooms on each floor, often with a small dressing or powder room attached. The interior of the house was panelled in wood, all of it pine, either from Scotland, or Scandinavia, and the only hard wood in the house was the banister of the staircase. The floors were also pine boards scrubbed with sand and, curiously, also with beer, to produce a clean matt finish.

Some important factors caused the house to sag internally provoking subsequent and extensive conservation work to refresh and recreate the interior. Structural problems had stemmed from previous construction work carried out by the Victorians who had built new inside walls which they'd then broken through to create extra doors. There had also been considerable subsidence when London's water table had risen as manufacturing in the capital had declined by the second half of the 20th century. The addition of a heavy roof which had been installed even earlier didn't help the structure of the house either. The house needed a hidden steel corset to ensure that the house would be stable, if not level. Sadly the fireplace surrounds had all been stolen, but the early 19th century cooking stoves remained and were faithfully restored. The lathe and plaster was renewed and the external walls were pulled in to tie in with the inner panelling with many small steel joists. Twenty eight layers of paint on the panelling were analysed and the colour nearest to the time of Franklin was selected while in Franklin's parlour a layer of varnish was detected as being of Franklin's time in the house. It is supposed that he would have had this done in order to improve the radiance of the candlelight.

In the sixteen years that Franklin lived at 36 Craven Street, the place became more than mere lodgings and more a home away from home for him and initially his son and their two servants, while he worked in the capital as Agent for the Assembly of Pennsylvania. He rented the four rooms on the first and second floors from the widowed landlady Mrs Stevenson who was believed to have had 'experience of the habits of Colonial Gentlemen' and who accepted the party warmly. He forged a friendship with her and her daughter Polly that was to prove great and lifelong. He left London only when the signs of conflict between the Colonies and the Mother Country became ominous, in March 1775.

Apart from china and table linen for entertaining guests, Franklin would have had little of his own furniture in Craven Street. There are very few descriptions of the furnishings or layout of the rooms, so most of the restorer's knowledge is based on conjecture, but Franklin plainly enjoyed shopping as records survive of many items he bought in London to send across the Atlantic to furnish a new house in Philadelphia. So it is likely that he did keep some things in Craven Street to enable him to entertain guests and appear to be a respectable "middling" man. The standard small Georgian house would have had Scotch or perhaps Turkish carpets, single ruched curtains covering shuttered windows. There were probably prints on the walls, as these were becoming very popular, especially unauthorised copies of Hogarth's moralistic series. We know Franklin had a portrait of his wife Deborah and that a small portrait by Mathew Pratt was sent across and copied by Benjamin Wilson to match the one hung in his Philadelphia house. The original work was stolen by the British when they occupied Philadelphia in 1778.

There was a suggestion initially that the house be refurnished and drawings were made to illustrate how the rooms would look. This illustration is of Franklin's parlour, and features many of the normal, middle class fashions in furnishings. If this is a good representation, then indeed it would seem that Franklin enjoyed a very comfortable home in London.

Since no original furniture survived, and because the 18th century spaces and rooms were so atmospheric in their spare beauty, the Benjamin Franklin House team decided not to furnish them in order to let them tell their own story. Thus the very small spaces are a canvas today for various events, primarily the Historical Experience show, a drama, which moves from room to room revealing the issues that concerned Franklin during his significant residence in the city. There is a Student Science Centre floor dedicated to Franklin's London science, which provides weekly free outreach to schools. Overall this is an inspiring monument to a compelling historical figure that's not to be missed.

TALKING TO DAVIDSON

Richard, how did you come to work as a furniture designer and manufacturer?

Richard: Whilst studying something completely unrelated at college in Brighton, I used to wander The Lanes that, in those days, were crammed with antique shops of all descriptions. I was fascinated by what I saw and also by the way antique dealers seemed to carry out their business. Rather than face my mother head on I wrote to her whilst she was spending the summer in the South of France, telling her of my intention to drop college and become an antique dealer.

Antique dealing is a fantastic way to earn a living and each day is different - you never know what treasures you are going to stumble upon. At that time it was possible to find wonderful pieces of furniture every week from dealers and auction rooms scattered all over the country.

It was around the early part of the nineties that I began to feel the need to create my own designs and this was combined with the view that the antique industry was going to face increasing challenges over the coming years. Our initial output was low key but over the next two or three years demand for our creations began to expand rapidly and my days of antique dealing were over.

How does Davidson work today?

Richard: The company has grown considerably in the last few years and we have been fortunate to remain remarkably busy during these difficult economic times. We believe it is our firm commitment to the highest levels of quality and craftsmanship that has seen the company thrive. Whilst materials such as veneers and handles are increasingly purchased from abroad, all our furniture is made in the UK. From initial veneer selection through to the finished product, the furniture is quality controlled through every stage of production up to the point of delivery and installation. We are very proud of our administrative structure which ensures that everything is delivered to the agreed delivery date.

Describe the Davidson furniture style?

Alexandra: Our furniture is based on classic lines which ultimately stand the test of time. Our aim is to create something that is beautiful to look at, that is constructed and polished with expertise but that is also practical to use, whether it be in a home, a boardroom, a luxury hotel or a superyacht.

What are your influences and what eras do you draw upon?

Alexandra: Currently we mainly draw our influence from the 20th century and more precisely the period from the 1930's and 1940's. However, much of the furniture designed during this period is in itself influenced by earlier periods. Our furniture is no exception but it has very much a contemporary interpretation, suited to today's needs.

Tell us about the recent opening of your new enlarged showroom?

Richard: We recently moved into a much larger showroom at the Design Centre where it is possible to showcase a far broader spectrum of our furniture. As the Design Centre itself begins a period of expansion, further development is in the pipeline.

Other than the showroom, have there been any other recent developments?

Alexandra: To coincide with the recent opening of the showroom, we have launched an improved, easy to navigate website which showcases a new collection of dining, console and occasional tables as well as dining chairs and side cabinets. This is the best tool to illustrate our full portfolio since not all of the furniture can be present at the Design Centre. With modern media advances we are keen to keep our fans and clients informed with regular news and updates and we encourage them to sign up to our newsletter mailing list and even follow us on Facebook or Twitter!

What does the year ahead hold in store?

Richard: Having moved to a larger showroom, our main focus for the year ahead is product development. This year you can expect many new pieces.

Can you tell us about any projects you are currently working on?

Richard: We are working on many interesting projects at the moment across the UK and from all corners of the globe. London is of course prominent within the UK but increasingly we are making deliveries to many diverse parts of the country. Luxury hotels such as the Four Seasons and the Ritz Carlton form an important part of our work as well as furniture for the world's leading superyacht interior designers.

Emerging markets for Davidson have been with Russian clients living in the UK as well as in Moscow and Saint Petersburg. Amongst the European market, Switzerland has been the most prominent. We have also had great success in Nigeria as well as some of the smaller countries bordering Saudi Arabia. We were particularly proud to send a large shipment to Syria recently; our first to this country.

What would be your dream project?

Alexandra: As a manufacturer we are constantly working on many projects at one time. Whether the project is large or small it is always a great bonus if the interior designer or their client has a clear idea of what they want. Having said that, our team of designers have endless patience and we are more than happy to spend time providing guidance drawn from our extensive experience and library of drawings.

What are the essentials that in your opinion transform a house into a home?

Richard: In my personal view it is the person living in the house that transforms a house into a home, however good a job the interior designer has done. It is the personal touches that give a home heart and soul. To some it comes easily and naturally – maybe it is the presence of a pet, a vase of flowers or even a bit of clutter. When combined with beautiful objects, pictures acquired over a period and of course wonderful furniture, a house can be transformed into a home!

How would you define the term luxury?

Richard: Whatever turns you on!

What are your personal luxuries?

Richard: Time to chill out with my border terrier.
Alexandra: My most precious moments of the day are my early morning walks with my Molly [Alexandra's dog!] This is one of the only opportunities I have during the day when I can focus my thoughts upon myself and be just a little bit selfish! An ultimate luxury is an hour's session of reflexology. You just can't beat it.'

Do you foresee any particular trends emerging in furniture design?

Richard: Without doubt it is the choice of materials that is going to influence furniture design in the coming years. Already certain timbers are becoming harder to source for ecological reasons. There are some companies that are producing engineered veneers that are becoming increasingly convincing and whilst this company has not used this type of product to date, it may be something to consider in the foreseeable future. As designers we will need to source innovative new materials and the possibility now to overlay wooden products with metallic finishes, of all descriptions, is an exciting prospect.

I think the key to all this is not to have a closed mind.

SHELLEY SAFARI INTERVIEW

How would you define or explain what you do? You do more than design interiors, it could be said you are a coach, a personal advisor even a psychological profiler, whose expertise and eye for detail enable you to customise a person's precious living space with great effect. Is this accurate?

Designing your home should be a fun and enjoyable experience...I work with this foremost in mind. It's a very personal process and by being perceptive and insightful to my clients' wants and needs, I provide a calm yet exhilarating journey from start to finish. I like to work closely with my clients, giving me time to really get to know them... and them me! And to understand what it is they actually want. Many people have an eye for style and know roughly what they like and dislike, so for some, it's just a question of guidance, suggestion and pulling the design together for a perfect and rewarding result which really reflects their own individuality. Occasionally my clients will give me a completely free rein (usually if they are overseas) but my favourite projects are when designing a home becomes a 'partnership' between me and my client...I guess I'm 'your best friend who just happens to be an interior designer'

What do you feel is the most important 'starting point' in any design?

Art! To me art is an intrinsic part of any design conception. It is a vital element, the 'heart' of any room. When you begin with the art you can create a beautiful and meaningful space inspired by the general 'feel' of an artwork rather than designing an entire room first and then trying to find an artwork to match your cushions after! I offer art consultancy and work with major international art galleries and experts, having direct access to hundreds of artists, sculptors and photographers around the world. 'Good' art need not be expensive, my sources range from the affordable hundreds... to the masters... and the hundreds of thousands. We can also offer commissioned work which provides great scope for colour and dimension, and commission bespoke sculptures. With such a large and diverse range of talent, the possibilities are endless!

What are the essentials that in your opinion transform a house into a home?

Lighting/mirrors/warmth and the ability to feel 'at home' in even the most stylish and seemingly 'pristine' environment. We all want a beautiful home, but we also need to be able to actually 'live' in it! Children, pets, parties.... all those elements of 'destruction' need to be taken into consideration at the beginning of any project. I also think that items which are of sentimental or personal value to the client should be incorporated into the design somehow. This is vital because a 'home' should be just that... 'a home!'.

What brought you to this particular point in your professional life?

A couple of years ago I came to a turning point in my life when I had to decide what I really wanted to do professionally. I had been developing properties for myself for many years and it had always been a passion and labour of love with each property. Becoming an interior designer seemed the most obvious and best way to fulfill my love of property design and is by far the best choice I have ever made!

would you say you have a particular style or signature? Or do you adapt to the person whose space you are creating and adorning?

I don't really have a particular style or signature as I am rather fickle when it comes to style in the sense that I can be in love with several trends or genres at once and constantly change my 'favourites'. I think this versatility helps when adapting to my clients' needs as I'm always bursting with several ideas all at once!

Can you tell us about any projects that you are currently working on?

My favourite project coming up is a beautiful country house in the home counties which I've been commissioned to start this spring. It will be a blank canvas and I'm very excited about the amazing opportunities to use and to integrate the lovely original features of the property into the design

What would be your dream interiors project?

Most definitely an Art Deco home. To be given carte blanche to faithfully reconstruct an interior using original furniture and, where possible, original fabrics and wallpapers. That, and perhaps a villa in Bali (my most cherished place right now!) Having rooms without walls provides all sorts of unusual and interesting design alternatives!

What are the preferred materials that you use across your designs?

I like to find unusual elements that add a subtle difference to an otherwise classic or mainstream look. For example, the alcove light features I recently designed are handmade and totally transformed the room they were placed in. Sometimes, just a simple strip of salmon skin across a cushion can create a unique point of interest. I love glass and natural woods, leather, silk and velvets. I'm extremely tactile even when shopping for clothes. I will run my hands over almost every garment just to feel the texture.

How would you define the term luxury?

Everyone's definition of luxury is so different and very personal. I would say luxury is anything that you get a buzz looking at... every time! Something that you feel a pleasure in possessing and which gives you constant joy

What are your personal luxuries?

Time! there seems to be so very little of it! If I find an extra unexpected ten minutes in which to just relax and have a coffee and be 'me' that is a total luxury! Other than that I would have to say flowers, my electric blanket and my beautiful bottles of various shapes, sizes and colours in my bathroom , oh, and my sheepskin rug in front of the fire which is also my cat's favourite luxury!

Do you foresee any particular trends emerging in interior design / furniture design?

As with all fashion, interior design is generally cyclical, but the impact on what we are able to create and design is very much influenced by the constant progression of technology within the textile and manufacturing industries. With consistently faster technology opening up new avenues of media integration into our everyday lives and homes, there are always new, exciting and innovative ideas to explore and implement.

What sort of hobbies do you do in your spare time (if you have any!)

I paint - not professionally, but just for fun. It was always a passion of mine and recently re-kindled after a visit to the Far East which inspired me so much that on my return from the airport I didn't even unpack but just ran to my local art shop, grabbed a canvas and started painting. I didn't leave my apartment for the whole weekend! My daughter who is only six, seems to have been inspired too, so now we argue over whose paint brushes are whose and she 'borrows' my canvases. The results are often amazing and most probably better than mine! I also teach kick boxing (Thai boxing to be precise), I'm a third dan and have been training for years. It keeps me fit and it's a great 'de-stresser'!

Where do you see yourself in the next 5 to 10 years?

A - Hmm... actually not far from where I'm at right now! I'm loving every moment..!

TALKING
TO TIM GOSLING

How did you come to be working as an interior / furniture designer?

I started off training as a Theatre Designer at Central St Martins which was amazing. It encompassed designing furniture, rooms, castles, landscapes – in fact all wonderful aspects of life which you had to draw from in order to be able to tell the story without anything being present.

Describe the 'Gosling' style?

The best way to describe the Gosling style, when all the designs are so individual, is Classical – inspired by Architecture. The styles of Architecture that we base our designs on range from the Renaissance through to Empire, Art deco, and 20th Century contemporary architecture.

What are your influences, and what eras do you draw upon?

I personally adore the 1930's and 1940's because of the explosion of delicate materials combined with the ability to challenge so many different styles of building to create what still looks today so ahead of its time. Furniture designers like Charles Rennie Mackintosh, Jacques-Emile Ruhlmann, Jean Michel Frank, and Armand Rateau.

Can you tell us about any projects that you are currently working on?

We are working on the most wonderful house in North London, designing it from scratch. The challenge is to balance the furniture with the architecture and then design the furniture as bespoke pieces specifically for the project. It's magical as it's a development so we have free range to create the most beautiful 40's inspired interiors.

What would be your dream interiors project?

I adore designing Libraries. For me the joy of combining history, books and design is the most exciting thing ever.

What are your favourite materials that you use across your designs?

In the last year or two we have been pushing the boundaries of wrapping vellum and printing onto it. It's such a versatile material and apart from a few book binders left in this country, it is a rare and valuable skill to be able to harness.

What are the essentials that in your opinion transform a house into a home?

Great lighting, a strong and distinct idea, and attention to detail.

How would you define the term luxury?

Luxury is a term that has been so over used recently. In my view it really is the TIME taken to create something with a client and the TIME taken to be able to create something totally unique.

What are your personal luxuries?

My personal luxury is being able to find the time to sketch and draw buildings. I know it's a strange one, but for me the sense of being able to capture something in spirit just by using markings on a page is wonderful.

Do you foresee any particular trends emerging in interior design / furniture design?

Looking ahead and in these days of being financially astute, I think the trend is to move towards the best quality money can buy. It's no longer a throwaway society. We are moving into a world once more where people care that something is made well and feel they can hand it down to future generations .After all, how 'Eco Friendly ' can you be - to make something that will last for 300 years?

ANNABELLA NASSETTI LTD AND AN BUILDING & MAINTENANCE LTD.

266 Fulham Road,
London, SW10 9EL
Email: fr@abnassetti.com
Website: www.abnassetti.com
Tel: +44(0)845 262 3456

ANNA CASA INTERIORS

Design Centre Chelsea Harbour,
South Dome-2nd Floor - Unit 2.24,
Lots Road, London, SW10 0XF
Email: info@annacasa.net
Website: www.annacasa.net
Tel: +44(0)20 7352 8353

BENJAMIN FRANKLIN HOUSE

36 Craven Street,
London, WC2N 5NF
Email: info@benjaminfranklinhouse.org
Website: www.benjaminfranklinhouse.org
Tel: +44(0)207 839 2006

BISQUE

244 Belsize Road,
London, NW6 4BT
Website: www.bisque.co.uk
Tel: +44(0)20 7328 2225

BRAHM INTERIORS

2 Motcomb Street,
London, SW1X 8JU
Website: www.brahminteriors.com
Tel: +44(0)20 7235 2372
Fax: +44(0)20 7235 2372

BROOSK SAIB

Email: broosk@broosk.com
Website: www.broosk.com
Tel: +44(0)20 8788 5130

CAROLYN TREVOR

Email: carolyn@tlastudio.com
Website: www.tlastudio.co.uk
www.carolyntrevor.co.uk
Tel: +44(0)207 7376181

CASA FORMA LIMITED

9 Princes Gate Mews,
London, SW7 2PS
Website: www.casaforma.co.uk
Tel: +44(0)20 7584 9495
Mob:+44(0) 7958 753 164
Fax:+44 (0) 20 7584 4046

CHARLIE YORK LTD

Email: jr@charlieyork.com
Website: www.charlieyork.com
Tel: +44 (0) 7597 564 310

COLLECTION PIERRE LTD

46 Bourne Street,
London, SW1W 8JD
Email: info@collectionpierre.com
Website: www.collectionpierre.com
Tel: +44(0)207 730 9020
Mobile: +44(0) 773 228 5984
Fax: +44(0) 207 730 9020

DAVIDSON LONDON

1/19 Design Centre,
South Dome,
Chelsea Harbour,
London, SW10 0XE
Website: www.davidsonlondon.com
Tel: +44(0)20 7751 5537

ENGLISH GEORGIAN

210 The Design Centre,
Chelsea Harbour,
London, SW10 0XE
Company No. 05900135
Website: www.englishgeorgian.com
Tel: +44(0)20 7351 4433
Fax: +44 (0)870 759 8382

FINE ENGLISH TRADING
COMPANY

Benedict Wormald
Email: enquiries@fineenglishcompany.com
Website: www.fineenglishcompany.com

FOLDE DESIGN LTD

21-23 Mossop Street,
London, SW3 2LY
Website: www.foldedesign.com
Tel: +44 (0) 207 589 9495

FORMS AT FORMWORK

forms@formwork.uk.com

FROMENTAL

The Saga Centre
326 Kensal Road
London, W10 5BZ
Tel UK: +44 (0) 203 410 2000
Tel US: +1 212 759 7888
Email: info@fromental.co.uk
Website: www.fromental.co.uk

GAVIN JACKSON LTD

Northfield House,
11 Northfield End,
Henley on Thames,
Oxfordshire, RG9 2JG
Email: deisgn@gavinjacksonarchitects.com
Website: www.gavinjacksonarchitects.com
Tel: +44(0)845 604 8455

GEORGE SMITH

George Smith Furniture and Fabrics
587-589 Kings Road
London, SW6 2EH
Tel: +44 (0) 207 384 1004
Fax: +44 (0) 207 731 4451
Web: www.georgesmith.co.uk

GIBSON MUSIC

Rachel Charles,
Unit 8 The Broomhouse, 50 Sulivan Road
London, SW6 3DX
Email: info@gibson-music.com
Website: www.gibson-music.com
Tel: +44 (0)20 7384 2270
Fax: +44(0)20 7731 1580

GODRICH INTERIORS

2A Farm Lane Trading Centre,
101 Farm Lane,
London, SW6 1QJ
Email: info@godrichinteriors.com
Website: www.godrichinteriors.com
Tel: +44(0)20 7386 8986
Fax: +44(0)20 7386 8633

GOSLING

Sycamore House,
4 Old Town,
London, SW4 0JY
Email: info@tgosling.com
Website: www.tgosling.com
Tel: +44(0)20 7498 8335

INTERIORS WITH ART LTD

Shailja Vohora and Sanjay Sharma,
13 Southcombe Street,
Kensington,
London, W14 0RA
Email: shailja@interiorswithart.com
Tel: +44 (0)207 602 7999
Fax: +44(0)207 348 3989

ISABELLA WOLFE

Website: www.isabellawolfe.com
Email: info@isabellawolfe.com
Tel: +1 646 476 2996

LIVING IN SPACE

43 England's Lane,
London, NW3 4YD
Email: anita@living-inspace.co.uk
ryan@living-inspace.co.uk
Website: www.living-inspace.co.uk
Tel: +44(0)20 7586 4747

LORCA DESIGN BY ELENA KARAMAN KARIĆ

Email: office@lorca-deisgn.com
Website: www.lorca-design.com
Tel: +381(11) 3676224

NUTTALL

No 2 Pond Place,
London, SW3 6QJ
Email: enquiries@nutallhome.com
Website: www.nutallhome.com
Tel: +44(0)20 7584 8989

R INTERIORS

Unit C10 The Depot,
2 Michael Road,
London, SW6 2AD
Email: info@rinteriors.net
Website: www.rinteriors.net
Tel: +44(0)20 7384 9284

SHARON MARSTON

Studio F31 & F34A,
Parkhall Studios,
40 Martell Road,
London, SE21 8EN
Email: info@sharonmarston.com
Website: www.sharonmarston.com
Tel: +44 (0)208 670 4644

SHELLEY SAFARI

12 Allen Mansions,
Allen Street,
Kensington,
London, W8 6UY
Email: info@shelleysafari-interiordesign.com
Website: www.shelleysafari-interiordesign.com
Tel: +44 (0)7850 190412

SONITE INNOVATIVE SURFACES CO. LTD

Sonite Showroom,
Crystal Design Center (CDC) Building D110,
1420 Soi Latphrao 87 (Juntrasuk) Praditmanutham Rd,
Klongjun Bangkapi, Bangkok 10240, Thailand
Email: internationalmarketing@sonitesurfaces.com
Website: www.sonitesurfaces.com
Tel: +66 2935 5594, Fax: +66 2935 5883

VIOLET AND GEORGE

Studio 2A,
101 Farm Lane,
London, SW6 1QJ
Email: info@violetandgeorge.com
Website: www.violetandgeorge.com
Tel: +44(0) 20 7386 3273

PHILIP MICHAEL WOLFSON

Email: info@wolfsondesign.com
UK Tel: +44 (0) 207 229 3221
US Tel: +1 917 421 9616

Acknowledgements

Thanks go to Quintessentially Publishing for drawing together all pieces of the jigsaw with the expertise of talented Marijus Burokas who has yet again created another stunning book, Leanne Simpson, Head of Design for her all seeing eye, to Daisy and the team at Icicle for all their hard work with printing the book, to Sophie Walker for her words of wisdom and for composing some beautiful pieces and to each and every designer who was featured in this book for their cooperation and input. We are proud to have worked with you all.